# OUTWARD BOUND

# BACKPACKER'S HANDBOOK

**Also available**
Outward Bound Canoeing Handbook
Outward Bound First Aid Handbook
Outward Bound Map and Compass Handbook
Outward Bound Orienteering Handbook
Outward Bound Rock Climbing Handbook
Outward Bound Sailing Handbook
Outward Bound Walker's Handbook

# OUTWARD BOUND
# BACKPACKER'S HANDBOOK

## Peter Barnes

WARD LOCK

**A WARD LOCK BOOK**
First published in the UK in 1995
by Ward Lock
Wellington House
125 Strand
London WC2R 0BB

A Cassell Imprint

Distributed in Australia by
Capricorn Link (Australia) Pty Ltd
2/13 Carrington Road, Castle Hill, NSW 2154

**British Library Cataloguing-in-Publication data**
A catalogue record for this book is available from the British Library

ISBN 0-7063-7363-4

Line illustrations: Kevin Maddison
Front cover photograph: Stephen Whitehorne
Back cover photograph: Mark Allen Publishing
Typesetting: Penny Mills
Printed and bound in Finland by Werner Söderström Oy

The author would like to thank Sue Towson for all her help and encouragement.

# Contents

# About Outward Bound®

*The Outward Bound Trust provides high-quality courses in a range of exciting outdoor activities. Our fully qualified instructors maintain the highest standards of tuition, and our safety record is second to none. Everyone who takes an Outward Bound course enjoys a rewarding and memorable experience, the benefits of which will last a lifetime.*

Outward Bound courses have been available in Britain since 1941. The original courses were the outcome of a meeting between Kurt Hahn, the educator, and Lawrence Holt, the owner of a shipping line. The marriage of the worlds of education and business is a vital feature of the Outward Bound movement. The courses are both a valuable adjunct to formal education and an important part of career development.

From its beginnings in Britain the Outward Bound movement has spread throughout the world, with 38 centres in 23 countries.

A typical course in the UK lasts from one to three weeks and may be based at one of our five national centres or take the form of an expeditionary journey by foot or by sailing boat in a wilderness setting. We run courses for all age groups, from 14 to 70!

The Outward Bound Trust also works directly with industry in designing programmes to help companies through periods of change. This may involve developing leadership skills for young managers or assisting in building cohesive teams. The courses balance challenging outdoor tasks with reflection and review. They are specially designed so that participants can always translate what they gain from a course back to their working environment.

After an Outward Bound experience, people discover many positive attributes about themselves. They become more confident; they learn to share; to lead and to follow; to understand their own strengths and to work together as a group. By safeguarding each other, they form bonds of trust. They discover that many problems can be solved only with the co-operation of all members of a group.

To find out more about Outward Bound courses or to request a brochure, please contact us at the address below:

Outward Bound Trust
PO Box 1219
Windsor
Berkshire SL4 LXR

Tel (01753) 731005

*Michael Hobbs*
Outward Bound Trust

# Introduction

There can be few activities which are as rewarding as being self-contained and exploring the countryside knowing that you have the equipment, capability and knowledge to complete your chosen journey. That journey might be across the foothills of the Himalayan mountains, through the jungles of Borneo, exploring the splendour of the North American Rockies, the wilderness of the Sinai Desert in Egypt, or walking a coastal footpath in southern England. The essence of the journey is the same: you have your home on your back and the world at your feet.

I have completed all of the journeys above and can honestly say that I have enjoyed the simplest amongst them as much as the hardest. Your journey is what you make it and the first requirement is having the skills to be comfortable and safe. This book is intended to point you in the right direction.

---

**By the end of the book you will know:**

---

- How to choose, plan and organize your journey.

- The right equipment and clothing for your intended trip.

- How to choose and use a tent, or any alternatives that might be suitable.

- How to decide what stove to take and how to use it both efficiently and safely as well as what food to cook on it.

- How to use a map and compass and how to navigate in both good weather and bad.

- The right ways to walk and carry loads over different types of ground.

- How to recognize and avoid dangers when out backpacking and what to do should you get into trouble.

---

Whilst this book is here for you to refer to, it is far better if you spend some time learning the various skills before setting off on your first backpacking trip. For example: at night in the pouring rain is not the place to start reading the instructions on how to put up your tent. It would be far better to have practised putting it up in the garden at home so that you know how it should be done. Apply the same principle to this book: by all means take it with you for reference but practise the skills beforehand. Likewise, start on a trip well within your capabilities and then progress to the harder stuff – if you want to progress, that is. There is nothing wrong with a walking career spent entirely on footpaths if that is what you enjoy.

Although this book is a complete guide to backpacking in itself, bear in mind that there are other books in the Outward Bound series which cover specific areas in greater detail. The relevant ones are the *Map and Compass, First Aid* and *Walker's* handbooks.

I do not want to preach over-caution but you should always remember that there are few activities which carry as much personal responsibility as being away from civilization and dependent on your own skills. In the words of that great mountaineer, Edward Whymper: 'Look to each step with prudence.' Nowhere is this more important than when the great moment arrives and you take others on their first backpacking trip. Whilst there are few things as magical as introducing others to the great outdoors and enjoying their new pleasure as others once enjoyed yours, bear in mind that a badly led trip can be as devastating as a good trip can be wonderful. Know your own limitations and those of your group.

But do not let this warning put you off – the only way you will find those limits is to get out there and do it. In all probability your walking career will be full of moments to savour.

# 1

## Planning a trip

### Initial planning

The initial idea for your trip might be a long-standing one or might have come from a wide range of sources, such as a magazine article, a TV show or a picture in a book. Whatever the inspiration, there will always be a number of factors that need to be taken into consideration.

### *Time*

The first is the time available and whether the trip is feasible in the time you have available. Chapter 6 will show you how to work out the time for the actual walking part of the trip but you also need to work out other time factors such as getting to and from your walk.

### *Transport*

This element of getting to and from your walk is the next consideration: is it practical? Ideally you simply walk out of your door and walk in a circular route back back to the start, but that is a rare possibility. Most of us not only have to get to the start of the walk but also have to return from the end of it. The easy solution is to take two cars and leave one at the walk's finish to take you back to the start. Even better is to pick a circular route. However, these options are not always available and in any case it is often nice to make your trip more of a journey and utilize public transport. This might be quite restricted in wilderness areas and you will certainly want to plan the finish of the walk carefully so that you do not miss the weekly bus home!

## Cost

The next factor is cost: can you afford it? Whilst backpacking is a wonderfully cheap activity there are costs to be considered. What are the transport costs? Are there permits to be bought? What is the cost of food and fuel? Can you afford to buy any gear you might need?

## Size of group

A major consideration is how many people will be going on the trip. There is a minimum group size for safety: with four people, if anything should happen to one of the group somebody can stay with the casualty whilst two go for help. In reality you will often walk in groups smaller than this or even, once experienced, by yourself, but in the beginning keep the group size within safe limits. If there are more than six or seven in a party, the group spirit starts to get lost and the group becomes an intrusion into the environment.

## Right of access

Almost every country in the world places legal restrictions on where and when you can walk. This is in addition to the time of the year when it is sensible, or even possible to walk in certain places.

To write in detail about every area you might want to go to would take up volumes and in any case be out of date as soon as it was printed. To find out: consult local guide books, read magazine articles, telephone the local tourist authorities or park offices. There will always be someone who can tell you. Incidentally, Sweden is thought to be the only country on earth where people have the right to roam anywhere – within reason.

## UK

The access laws in the UK are complicated and vary from place to place. National parks are national in their significance, not in their ownership, and much of the land is privately owned. Check with any national park office for the restrictions on access in their area and the UK in general. Also, great swathes of the British countryside are still closed for large parts of the year so that the owners can shoot at the wildlife in 'peace'. In general marked public footpaths and bridleways should always be open for public use.

## Continental Europe

Whilst the wild European areas such as the Alps are much less restricted there are still some restrictions, notably on 'wild' camping. Discover which local authority is responsible, or ask at the mountain guides' office in the area, and find out the rules.

## USA and New Zealand

The great wilderness areas of the USA and New Zealand are some of the most tightly controlled in the world. In many cases areas are closed for certain seasons of the year and often you will need to contact the park authorities in order to get a permit firstly to be in the area and secondly to camp, if it is allowed at all. Many trails will be marked, or blazed, with colours painted at intervals on trees and rocks. Often you will not be allowed away from these trails.

## *When to go*

As for chosing the time of year, it is easier to plan for the season and be prepared for whatever the weather brings. It may be that you have other criteria than the weather for choosing a particular season. Any right-minded person avoids Skye in Scotland during the summer because of the unbearable midges, for example. It may be that you want to avoid crowds, in which case the English Lake District, America's Grand Canyon or Chamonix in France at the height of the tourist season are not the places to visit. If you are committed to going backpacking in the summer, when of course the weather is usually at its best, a bit of research will repay you with 'unexplored' areas.

Do not always assume that the off-season means bad weather. If you are willing to take a chance, autumn and spring can provide some wonderful walking days – as can winter, of course, if you are prepared and equipped for harsher conditions. The biggest constraint is usually that the days are shorter, considerably so as you move further north, so the margin for error becomes less and less.

## Weather

Once you have decided when and where to go and that the transport is manageable, the cost is reasonable, the season is right and the access is not a problem, it is time to get down to the real planning. The first consideration for most people will be the weather.

### Forecasts

Weather forecasts are usually available for all but the most remote regions and it is essential to know how to interpret them.

Firstly, obtain a forecast that is as up to date as possible. Newspaper forecasts are of little use as they are already many hours out of date by the time they reach you. For example: if you want a forecast for Saturday, the Friday paper will be using information from Thursday – it will nearly two days old by the time you get out on your walk. However, a good paper will show a synoptic chart (figure 1.1). By following these charts over a few days you will be able to see how the weather is developing, which will give you a good indication for the days ahead.

A better forecast for everyday use is one that is updated regularly, especially if it specifically covers the area you want to visit. The forecasts on local television and radio are good because they are up to date but usually the best option is a 'weatherline' telephone service if available. These services are often operated by

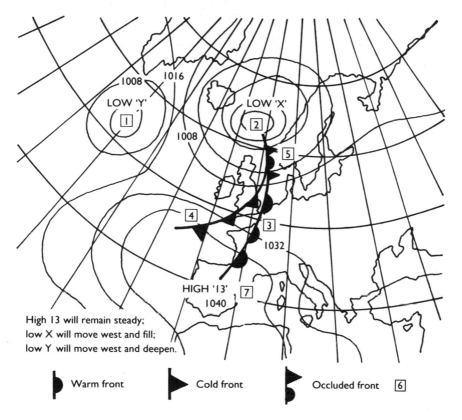

High 13 will remain steady;
low X will move west and fill;
low Y will move west and deepen.

▶ Warm front     ◣ Cold front     ◪ Occluded front   6

**1.1** A typical synoptic chart.

national parks and similar authorities or outdoor organizations; they are not only up to date but also very specific for the weather in the area of interest.

## Synoptic charts

When reading synoptic charts you are looking for two features and, more importantly, the way they are moving. The first feature is any area of low pressure, marked in figure 1.1 as areas [1] and [2]. These can usually be relied upon to bring bad weather, because of the associated fronts which travel around them (marked in the figure as [3], which is a warm front, and [4], a cold front). Sometimes these fronts can move together and form an occluded front [5].

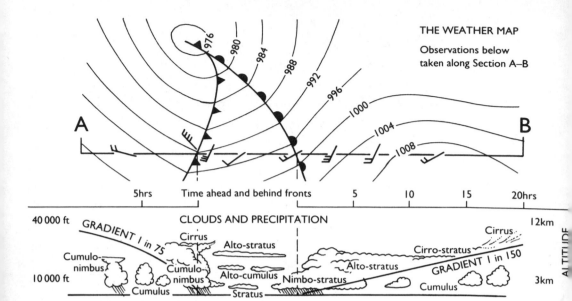

**1.2** A frontal system.

Lows and fronts mean wet weather but that information is useless unless you know in which direction they are moving. This is usually mentioned on the chart, as is what is happening to the pressure systems [6]. It is best if you can watch the charts over a few days to gather a picture of how the weather is developing, which is often according to a set pattern. In the UK, for example, it almost invariably comes in from the west because of the UK's position in relation to the air streams which move the weather around the globe.

The alternative to low pressure is, of course, high pressure [7]. High pressure systems bring good weather, although in winter it will be very cold. They can block lows from moving in and, when over land, they tend to 'hang around', which means that they often bring very settled weather.

It can be seen from figure 1.2 how the leading warm front brings a long period of drizzle or light rain whilst the following cold front will bring short but often heavy showers. Note that the high cirrus clouds which are a good indicator of an approaching front may be 15–20 hours ahead of the rain.

## Mountain weather

Mountainous areas can have profound effects on the behaviour of the weather. For example: it will usually be much wetter on the windward side of the mountains; indeed it is possible for one side of a mountain range to be wet whilst the other is a known dry area. More immediate effects are that the temperature will decrease as you climb higher: allow for a drop of 1°C (1.8°F) for every 150m (490ft) that you climb.

Wind is also affected, often dramatically, by the mountains. Ridges and high plateaux will always accelerate the speed of the wind as it 'squeezes' over the top. There will also be a noticeable increase in the speed of the wind where it is squeezed into small gaps, such as along high passes. This funnelling effect will often be enough to turn a gentle wind into a gale strong enough to make walking difficult.

On the coast you will generally find that steeply rising coastlines facing onshore air streams are very wet places.

## Other considerations

Some of what follows might seem more like planning an expedition to the far-flung corners of the earth rather than a weekend walking trip but the theory for both is the same; only the quantity varies. It is often the short, simple trips that go wrong because people forget things like matches or the tent pegs. Planning a trip is something that comes with experience but soon becomes as much a part of the trip as the walking itself.

### Equipment

Firstly, what equipment and clothing are you going to take (see Chapter 2) – and how much can you comfortably carry? A useful tip: when you get back, empty your sack out. If something was not used, ask yourself why, and if you cannot think of a decent reason do not take it again. Travel light.

If you are going abroad, take clothes that respect the local culture. Many villages in Nepal, for example, do not take kindly to skimpy western clothes being worn, a fact which is ignored by too many visitors.

Decide how many tents you are going to take and whether they are suitable, (see Chapter 3). Do you have enough spare pegs and other accessories?

Buy and pack your stove, fuel and food (see Chapter 4). Is it possible to carry all your food or are you going to be able to replenish your supplies? It is unlikely that you will want to carry more than three or four days' food. Is the food suitable? (Dehydrated food, for example, might be a problem in an area where water is hard to come by.) If you are travelling by air at any stage, remember that it is illegal to carry fuel; ensure that your chosen fuel is available where you are going. Do not forget the matches – and spares!

## Route planning

Start thinking about planning your route in detail. Are you sure you know all the potential hazards on your route? For example: are the rivers all crossable, and can you still get past them if it pours with rain?

It is also important to take into consideration a number of factors which might not occur to you initially, such as interest, timing and fitness.

### Planning an interesting route

Plan a route that has some intrinsic interest rather than being just a journey from A to B. Good use of your map will often point to a number of features, both natural and otherwise. Contour lines (see Chapter 5) show not only the slope of hills but also peaks which might stand out and provide good view points. Map symbols can provide a wealth of information on constructed features that might provide a good diversion or objective.

Use guide books and local organizations (see Appendix) when researching your route. Another good idea is to discover the meaning of some of the local names on your map. For example: 'Hafotty', which is often seen on Welsh maps, is the local word for summer farms used by shepherds in days gone by. Knowledge like this means that the ruined buildings which you pass become alive with local history.

## Time

Always allow more time than you expect to need. For a start, it is always better to finish early than to finish late and miss the last bus home. Secondly, extra time gives you more leisure to enjoy the walk and the sights around you. (A rushed walk I once did with my brother along Offa's Dyke – the ancient border between England and Wales – became little more than a blur of footpaths and stiles. If we had allowed a couple more days, the route could have been tackled at a far more leisurely pace and then we might actually have seen some of the sights.)

## Fitness

Never overestimate your own fitness and ability. Walking for three days or more does not compare with day walks, and your planning needs to allow for the fact that any long walk becomes tiring.

Until you have gained some experience and knowledge of your own ability, it would be sensible to plan a route that passes stopping points for public transport or to plot a circular route that can be curtailed by heading directly for the finish when you become worn out or run out of time.

## Route cards

You will need to let somebody know exactly where you are going, including planned alternatives. This information, in the form of a route card, should be left with a responsible person who knows what to do if your return is overdue. Route cards not only aid a potential rescue team but they also help you to make decisions about, and be able to follow, emergency routes and bad-weather routes, details of which should be on the cards.

The route card is not intended to be a substitute for taking a map on the hills but it can be used in a situation where you are cold, the wind and the rain are blowing down and it would be a nightmare to get out your map and compass and start working out bearings to the next point. Having them already worked out back in the comfort of your base is a great asset. You will, of course, still need to have your map out so that you can keep an eye on your check features as you pass them.

A typical route card is shown in figure 1.3. Note that the day is divided into legs, with the end of each one written down as a grid reference (see page 78) and description. Each leg should be short enough so that it can be done on a single bearing but not so long that you could lose track of where you are. The exception would be if you were following a major footpath or track where it would be a nonsense to treat each bend in the path as a separate leg. In this case, just give a general direction of the path and note any major check features.

Completing a route card before each walking trip requires you to work out the times for each leg and the overall day (see Chapter 6). In this way you will avoid any unpleasant surprises such as finding yourself still walking at midnight. When working out your timings, I would suggest that for every hour or so you add 5 minutes to allow time for the inevitable stops, and also allow time for lunch.

An alternative route might be a low-level one so that you could substitute it in the event of bad weather if your original route was at a high level. Escape routes should be quick, safe ways off the route that you can take in the event of a crisis. (It is a good idea to note the locations of the nearest public telephones here.)

Whenever you go on the hill, you should prepare at least two route cards. Take one with you and leave the other one with a responsible person who will know whom to give it to if you fail to return by the stated time.

# ROUTE PLAN

Date:------------------Members of party: -----------------------------------------------------------------------------------

Weather forecast: -----------------------------------------------------------------------------------------------------------------

Starting point reference:-------------------------Description: -----------------------------------Time: --------------

| to grid reference | Description (of target) | Direction | Distance | Time (for distance) | Height gain | Time (for height) | Total time | Description (of route and terrain) | Possible alternative route | Escape route |
|---|---|---|---|---|---|---|---|---|---|---|
| | | | | | | | | | | |
| | | | | | | | | | | |
| | | | | | | | | | | |
| | | | | | | | | | | |
| | | | | | | | | | | |
| | | | | | | | | | | |
| | | | | | | | | | | |

Finishing point reference: ------------------------   Estimated pick up time: -------------------------

Description ---------------------------------------   Estimated phone in time------------------------

**1.3** A typical route card.

Each year countless hours are spent by rescue teams looking for overdue backpackers without any real idea of where they should be searching. Route cards might seem like a hassle before a trip but might just turn out to be a life-saving investment.

# 2

## Clothing and equipment

Central considerations in compiling an equipment list are the need to be warm, dry, comfortable and safe. You also require the most efficient means of carrying your equipment. Whatever you carry, whether on your body or on your back, ensure firstly that it works, secondly that it is light and finally that you really do need it. Every ounce counts when you are backpacking.

.

## Basic clothing

Unless you are heading for a hot climate, your clothing requirements can be based around staying warm, dry and comfortable.

### *The layer system*

It has long been accepted that the way to keep warm and dry outdoors is to adopt a layer system that keeps the elements at bay, whisks the sweat away from your skin to keep you dry and traps air to keep you warm. Layers can also be removed or added in order to cope with varying conditions. The system is divided into a base layer, a warmth layer and a foul-weather layer.

### Base layer

This is the layer worn next to your skin. It is normally made up from polypropylene/nylon mixtures that will 'wick' moisture away from your skin. These clothes are vital as sweat next to your body will cool quickly and make you very cold when you stop. The top layer is usually a thin, long-sleeved top with or without a roll neck; a bottom layer of long johns is useful in winter. Some people wear the long johns as trousers, with shorts over them.

## Warmth layer

The top half of this layer usually consists of a shirt of some sort under a fleece or pile jacket or pullover. The main advice when choosing a fleece from the overwhelming selection on the market is that if it is really cheap you should be asking yourself why.

For the bottom half of this layer, avoid wearing denim jeans: they provide no warmth when wet and the thick seams will rub skin raw. Poly-cotton or fleece trousers are ideal. I tend to wear salopettes, which prevent your shirt riding up under a rucksack. Salopettes are very warm and cosy to wear but if you ever need to get them off in a hurry under several other layers you will curse the day you bought them!

## Foul-weather layer

This is where things suddenly start to get very expensive. What you are looking for is a layer that will do two things: keep out the cold, the wind and the rain; and let your perspiration escape. All waterproof garments manage the first requirement to a greater or lesser extent but the second requirement, known as breathability, is a different matter.

Traditional waterproofs are made with a totally waterproof material, usually nylon coated with polyurethane (PU), which works well at keeping you dry from the outside. However, as soon as you start to exercise, you will perspire and this type of garment can leave you very wet from the inside. This problem is overcome by using a wide range of sophisticated technologies to produce garments which breathe, in other words outside moisture is kept out whilst perspiration is allowed to escape. Some of the main trade names to look for are Gore-tex, Sympatex, Cyclone, Hydro Dry and Triple Point. These all work in different ways and have slightly different properties. When you come to make the decision about buying waterproofs, perhaps the biggest help is to listen to the experience of friends and do a lot of asking around.

## Double-P system

There is a recent innovation in outdoor clothing which many people are using in preference to the layer system. This is the Double-P system of clothing where the double Ps stand for Pertex and fibre Pile. In this system less layers are worn with the theory being that the fibre pile will stay warm against the skin even when wet. These clothes, of which 'Buffalo' are the biggest make, need to fit much tighter than conventional outfits.

## Making a choice

Choosing your basic clothing can be daunting in terms of both the range of products available and their prices. Always keep in mind what you want the garment to do and be honest with yourself. There is little point, for example, in buying a very expensive top-of-the-range mountain jacket if all you intend to do is walk on local trails. Likewise a cheap jacket from the local corner shop could be a major hazard if you were to wear it in the mountains in winter. Do not be fooled by superficial gimmicks but go for the essential features. Do your trousers really need eight pockets? Is the map pocket on the jacket large enough? Is the hood large enough? How long will the garment last? On this last point be aware that many breathable fabrics have a short useful life, sometimes as short as three years or less if you buy an inappropriate one. Things like the length of the jacket you use will be a personal choice but be practical. A modern fashion for short jackets has developed because advertisements tend to show them being worn by hard climbers on the mountains. You might not realise that mountaineers usually wear waterproof salopettes when wearing short jackets. It may be more appropriate for you to have a jacket which is long enough to keep you dry when you sit on the ground.

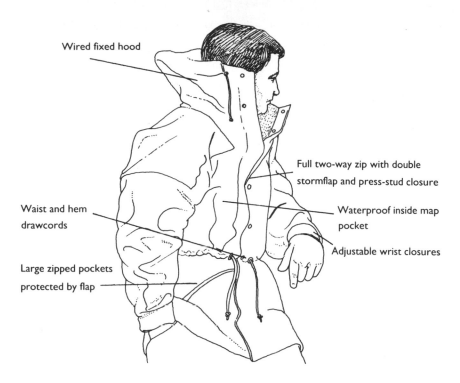

Wired fixed hood

Full two-way zip with double
stormflap and press-stud closure

Waist and hem
drawcords

Waterproof inside map
pocket

Adjustable wrist closures

Large zipped pockets
protected by flap

**2.1** Features of a waterproof jacket.

When you try clothes on, move around in them to ensure that they give a good fit. In particular, stretch your arms above your head and bring your knees up high to see if there are any tight areas. With top layers, bear in mind that you might want to put several other layers beneath them. Ensure that all zips are substantial and, if needed, will open in either direction. Waterproof trousers should have long zips enabling them to be put on whilst wearing boots.

## Hot climates

Care needs to be taken when choosing your clothing even if you are fortunate enough to be walking in a hot country. Under no circumstances should you walk in the sun without a hat on as you are inviting at best a pounding headache and at worst a very unpleasant dose of heat stroke. A wide-brimmed hat is absolutely essential; a baseball cap is better than nothing.

Shorts and vests or T-shirts are very comfortable but I prefer to avoid sunburn by wearing trousers and long-sleeved shirts in lightweight cotton or a modern synthetic equivalent. You never see the local population of desert countries anything less than fully covered.

The danger in hot climates is in being too casual: you still need to be prepared for everything that the local weather might throw at you. Nights can be very cold in hot regions and you might also be subjected to violent thunderstorms.

## Boots

There is now a wide and diverse range of boots on the market but essentially they can be split into several categories:

### Shoes and lightweight boots

Shoes designed for walking might be adequate for simple trail walking but they do not give any ankle support and should not be used on anything other than the flat. Lightweight boots are a step up from shoes and give a minimal amount of ankle support but they tend to be made of fabric and are not waterproof – I would not recommend them for off-trail walking.

### General walking boots

Medium weight, general purpose boots made of waterproofed leather or fabric are the choice of many backpackers. They should be substantial enough to give a good amount of support. Some of the fabric boots come with a Gore-tex inner which gives them a degree of waterproofing and breathability.

### Mountaineering boots

Mountaineering boots are made of either a heavier leather or plastic. They give extremely good support, largely owing to the

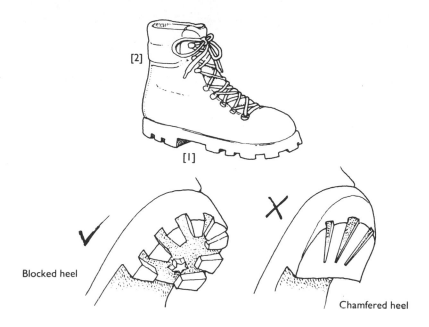

Blocked heel

Chamfered heel

**2.2** A typical general-purpose boot. Note the square-cut sole and heel [1] and generous ankle support [2].

fact that they are made rigid enough to be used with crampons. These boots are not comfortable for general walking purposes.

## Wellingtons

Walking 'wellies' or 'bog trotters' are essentially short wellington boots which are tighter fitting than usual and have walking soles. Although they give only a minimal amount of support, they are ideal for very wet ground.

---

**When you choose your boots look for the following features:**

---

- Well padded support around the ankles but beware of the fit being too tight against the Achilles' tendon.

- A reasonably rigid sole which does not bend too much either along the length of the boot or across its width. More than 2cm (1in) when holding the heel and pushing the toes up is too much.

- A substantial sewn-in tongue which will both keep water out and not slip around on top of your foot.

- A good chunky Vibram sole, square-cut along all the lower edge including the heel. Be very wary of any substitutes for the traditional sole – many of the newer lightweight materials do not grip at all in the wet. Avoid cut-away or rounded heels even if you are told that they make walking easier; this may be true but some people find that they make it difficult to get a secure foothold when descending steep grass slopes. The sole should feel solid and substantial, not soft and giving (which is another modern innovation supposedly for comfortable walking).

- A good fit is absolutely essential. As a rule, the boot needs to be just tight enough to hold your foot but not loose enough to slop around in. Try standing on your toes and seeing what happens. Your toes should not be at all squashed into the front of the boot. At the back there should be just enough room to squeeze a finger down behind your ankle.

- Ensure that both boots fit well. Even minor differences in the size of your feet could make themselves felt with unforgiving boots.

---

## Socks

Remember that the most expensive boots in the world will be uncomfortable if worn with cheap and nasty socks. A major cause of blisters is ill-fitting, wet or dirty socks; socks with large seams are also a menace. A lot of people still wear two pairs of socks but for many years now I have never worn more than a single pair. The choice is largely a personal one but you should never need to wear more than two pairs. Using insoles in boots is a good idea, especially the modern shock-absorbing type: not only can they help to give a good fit but they also provide a surprising amount of cushioning.

## Caring for boots

It is worth spending as much as you can afford on your boots; more than anything else they can make or break a walking trip. Care of boots should never be neglected and a good pair of boots, looked after well, can last a lifetime with the occasional resoling. Your boots should be washed after each trip and dried gently with the laces and insoles removed. Never dry boots rapidly in front of a fire or radiator as this will crack them. Follow the manufacturer's advice for which proofing to use.

## Gaiters

Gaiters for walking boots were originally designed to keep snow out but now many people never walk without them. Essentially there are three types: the normal calf-length version which covers the top of the boot, a short type which just goes around the ankle and a third version which completely encloses the boot.

Gaiters are useful for everything from keeping water and stones out of boots to keeping trousers clean. If you are considering the

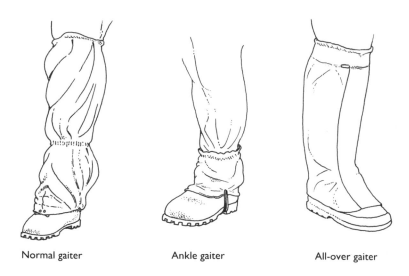

Normal gaiter      Ankle gaiter      All-over gaiter

**2.3** Types of gaiter.

all-over gaiter, which will keep your feet totally dry, ask yourself if you really need them. They can be very expensive and also the rubber rands which go under the boots can wear out very quickly. If you do decide to go for them, ensure that your boot is the type which will accept them. Personally I tend to wear ankle gaiters in snow or all-over gaiters in very wet country but otherwise I do not bother with them.

Do not make the classic mistake of tucking your waterproof trousers inside your gaiters. If you do, all the water will simply run down your legs and fill up your boots.

## Hats and balaclavas

You should never go walking without a hat. In winter it will keep your head warm and in summer it will protect your head from the sun.

A large percentage of body heat is lost from the head so it is sensible to wear a hat in cold conditions. Wearing one whilst in your sleeping bag can make a surprising difference, too. In winter go for a hat which covers your ears and will not flap around. If it has a peak, make sure that it is stiff.

You could substitute a balaclava for the hat but personally I dislike always wearing balaclavas and tend to take just a thin one that I can wear with the hat if it gets really cold. Beware of the traditional woollen hats and balaclavas: they can itch like crazy when you start to sweat.

In summer a wide-brimmed bush hat will be invaluable for keeping the sun at bay.

## Gloves

When choosing gloves, ask yourself whether they are suitable for your intended use. A good combination is a thin pair of warm gloves with a heavier pair of waterproof gloves to wear if the weather turns foul. Avoid gloves which do not cover the wrist unless you wear very long sleeves or use wristlets: you will be surprised how cold that bare strip of skin can get.

## Rucksacks

Along with your waterproofs and boots, it is your rucksack that dictates whether you will be comfortable whilst walking. In the shop it is difficult to tell if the sack really suits you, so seek the advice of friends who already own sacks. There are several main features to look for in a rucksack.

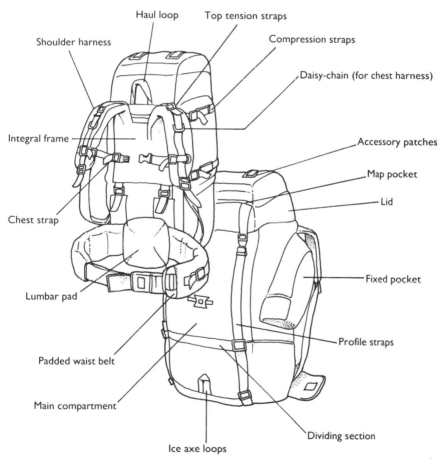

**2.4** Features of a rucksack.

## Size

Weight is rarely a problem with modern sacks but some older ones might be quite heavy.

Choose a sack which is larger than you need so that you have adequate capacity when you progress to bigger trips. Some sacks are adjustable in size, using a bellows system, but you should at least have compression straps so that you can pack the sack down tight after it is loaded. As a rough guide I would suggest 65 litres as the size needed for the average two or three day backpacking trip.

Although many rucksacks have a multitude of adjustments that can be made to them, it is still important that the sack fits you correctly. Most sacks will come in a variety of lengths and the correct length should be your priority when making a decision. Do not compromise on size or you will regret it later.

## Carrying straps, pockets and lids

There are essentially two sets of straps for carrying sacks: the shoulder straps and the waist strap. There is often a chest strap which brings the shoulder straps in closer together to give a better fit and help to spread the load. When carrying the sack, the waist strap should be sitting on top of your hips rather than around your waist. Although the actual balance is a personal choice, aim to have around a third of the weight on the waist strap. The waist strap should have substantial padding all round; the padding on the shoulder straps should be cut away from under the arms.

Pockets are a matter of personal choice but I would always recommend a large pocket in the lid for small items that you will need during the day. A good compromise is to have detachable pockets on the side so that you can use them when desired and also vary the capacity of the sack. Dividing the main sack into compartments is a gimmick with little real application.

The top of the sack should have a lid which will completely

cover it no matter how much has been packed inside. There should also be an extension to the sack which can be pulled over the opening to seal it. This extension is also useful if you ever want to use your rucksack as an improvised sleeping bag.

## Frames

The development of the internal frame has meant that the days of the pack frame have all but gone. There is now as big a variety of frames as there is of rucksacks but there is probably not a great deal to choose between them.

## Packing a rucksack

Novices never cease to be amazed by how quickly experts pack their sacks but it is simply a case of developing your own system and sticking to it. There are a number of simple guidelines which will help.

Firstly, no rucksack is waterproof so use a heavyweight plastic bag as a sack liner (a normal bin bag will not be substantial enough). If you want to be absolutely sure, wrap your sleeping bag and spare clothes in another bag as well. Remember that the lid pocket of the sack will not be waterproof either so it is prob ably not a good place to store your matches.

The rule to follow when packing your sack is 'last out – first in'. Place things such as your sleeping bag and spare clothes at the bottom of the sack where they can remain undisturbed until needed. Essential items such as your first aid kit need to be at the top. Perhaps the best place to pack your waterproofs is under the lid of the sack so that if it starts raining it is not necessary to undo the main compartment of the sack. The tent is more of a problem: when it is dry and easily folded it can go in the sack beside your lunch; however, on the second or third days when it has become wet it is often a good idea to leave it under the lid.

Ensure that your fuel bottle and stove are well wrapped in extra

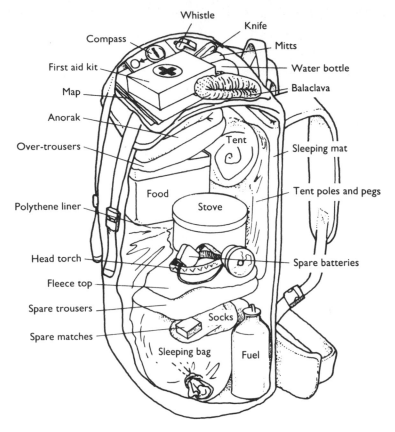

Whistle
Knife
Compass
Mitts
First aid kit
Water bottle
Map
Balaclava
Anorak
Tent
Over-trousers
Sleeping mat
Food
Polythene liner
Stove
Tent poles and pegs
Head torch
Spare batteries
Fleece top
Spare trousers
Socks
Spare matches
Sleeping bag
Fuel

**2.5** Packing a rucksack.

bags to protect your food and clothes from the smell of fuel. For the sake of balance, keep heavy items low and close to your back, though this is not always feasible and it is not so critical with modern sacks as it once was.

The last check is make quite sure that there is nothing sticking out which is going to dig into you. In figure 2.5 the sleeping mat has been folded and used to pad the back of the sack. It could also be formed into a lining tube within the sack, with everything else packed inside the tube. A third option is to roll it tightly and strap it to the outside of your sack.

Make it your goal to have as little as possible on the outside of the sack. There a risk that it will get damaged and anyway there is nothing more annoying to the group than the clatter of dangling mugs and cooking pots.

## Other Equipment

Tents, bivvy bags, sleeping bags and sleeping mats are discussed in Chapter 3, and food, stoves and fuel in Chapter 4 (don't forget to take a pan scourer). Trekking poles, crampons and ice axes are covered in Chapter 6.

### Torches

A torch and spare batteries are absolutely essential. When carrying a torch, reverse one of the batteries so that the positive terminals are together; in this way it cannot be switched on accidentally. If you are more serious about backpacking, think about investing in a head torch. These torches, which fit on the head with an elastic strap, are worth their weight in gold when you realize that you do not have enough hands to cook with in the dark.

### Emergency equipment

A whistle should be carried by every member of the group. It needs to be carried somewhere handy such as in the lid pocket. Having it buried in your first aid kit is no good if it is needed in a hurry. You should never blow your whistle unless it is an emergency.

> The INTERNATIONAL DISTRESS SIGNAL is six sharp blasts followed by one minute of silence. This pattern (six blasts and silence) should be repeated continuously as a location guide until help arrives. This distress signal can also be given by using a torch or shouting.

It is also important to carry a pencil and notebook (usually in your first aid kit). In addition to making notes, you might need to write an emergency message in a crisis, to be carried by whoever goes for help.

If tents are not being carried, each individual should have their own plastic survival bag. The use of such a bag as an emergency shelter is described in Chapter 8. It is sensible for a group to carry at least two bags that are big enough for two people.

## Knives

The Swiss army knife has never really been beaten as the most useful all-round tool when camping. There is no need to carry large knives or machetes unless your trip involves blazing trails or clearing bush. The big advantage of the Swiss army knife is that it contains all the little things that so easily get lost, like a can opener. Beware of cheap imitations; they will be a poor investment in the long run.

## Spares

Spare matches can be carried in an old film container together with a striker. You can never have enough spare matches.

Spare clothes should always be carried. On a day walk it is enough to carry a spare pair of socks and an extra sweater. For longer trips you need to carry a full change of clothes in case you get completely soaked. I tend to carry a spare set of thermal top and bottoms which I keep exclusively for sleeping in.

Although not every person in a group needs a map and compass, there should be at least a couple of spares in addition to the sets being used. The main map needs to be protected by either lamination or a map case.

Carry a small amount of spare food in case you get caught by nightfall or have to spend extra time on the hill. A few chocolate bars and some boiled sweets should be enough.

## Water bottles and flasks

I tend not to carry a water bottle as I always have a hot flask with me. However, many people like cold drinks when backpacking and it is a good idea to spend a bit of money and get a quality bottle which will serve you well. I do carry one of those foil bags that come out of wine boxes; they make excellent water carriers at the camp-site. On the subject of flasks, do not let the price of the metal unbreakable type put you off – they are worth every penny.

## Group gear

The gear that is carried between the members of the party should include a small spade for digging a toilet hole at the camp-site, a 30m (100ft) length of 9mm (0.3in) safety rope and an emergency shelter. The latter, which is simply a large piece of rip-stop nylon, is not strictly needed if members of the group are carrying tents or survival bags but it does make a good, quick shelter for all manner of stops.

## First aid kits

Every backpacker should carry a first aid kit. Each person will have their own favourite items but some are essential.

---

### Typical contents of a first aid kit:

---

- Plastic gloves (for AIDS and hepatitis protection).
- A small selection of gauze dressings.
- Antiseptic wipes and ointment.
- Antihistamine cream for insect bites.
- Plasters, or a roll of plaster.
- Zinc oxide tape.
- Crepe bandage.

- Two (or even three) triangular bandages.
- Safety pins.

## Weight of equipment

Finally, once you have decided exactly what you need, think again about weight. Almost nothing ruins a backpacking trip more than carrying too much on your back. A general guide is that no one should carry more than a third of their own body weight but this does depend a great deal on your own experience and ability.

Be totally ruthless where weight is involved. Do you really need a mountain tent which might weight 5kg (11lb), when a low-level tent weighing only 3kg (7lb) is enough? Do you really

Weight

**2.6** Carrying a packed rucksack correctly. Note that the weight of the sack is balanced vertically, not dropping back from the body. The sack itself is snug to the body, with the shoulder straps and belt well adjusted.

need two extra pullovers or three spare pairs of socks? Look closely at the stove you buy: having one which will boil water in five minutes is all very well but if it weighs 2kg (4lb) when one that boils water in twice the time weighs only half as much, then opt for the lighter one. The same applies with sleeping bags: get one which is appropriate rather than excessive and save another kilo or two of weight.

The biggest enemy of weight efficiency is the 'just in case' factor. Whilst you do need first aid kits, spare clothes and emergency shelters, avoid too much replication within a group. There is no point in everybody carrying a full first aid kit, for example.

If you think to yourself, 'This is heavy,' when you first pick up your packed rucksack, then think again. After a couple of days it will have become too heavy.

Figure 2.6 shows how to balance a rucksack correctly when you are walking.

# 3

## Tents and camping

### The tent

Not so many years ago, choosing a tent was a simple affair. It would be a ridge tent, probably with A-poles at each end; it would be made of waterproofed cotton and weigh half a ton, or at least feel like it after a night's rain.

Today, however, a bewildering array of tents is available but nearly all of them have certain features in common, as shown in figure 3.1.

### *Tent layers*

With the exception of single-skin Gore-tex designs, tents will have two layers: the inner tent and the fly sheet. The job of the fly sheet, or outer tent, is to provide weather-proofing. It will probably have guys attached for extra security; there will be a number of loops around the edge for pegs to go through; there will be at least one door and possibly a snow valance, which is a flap of material around the edge of the flysheet. The valance is useful on hard ground or in bad weather because rocks or snow can be piled on it, making the tent much more secure. The disadvantage is that it can freeze to snow; also, because it reduces the air flow around the tent, it can increase condensation.

The inner sheet will be of a lighter weight material, its function being to provide a dry 'room' within the tent. It does this by allowing condensation to pass out into the area between it and the fly sheet, thus preventing drips from forming. It should have a good sewn-in groundsheet, preferably one that curls up around the edges in a 'tray' style. One of the biggest weight savings to be

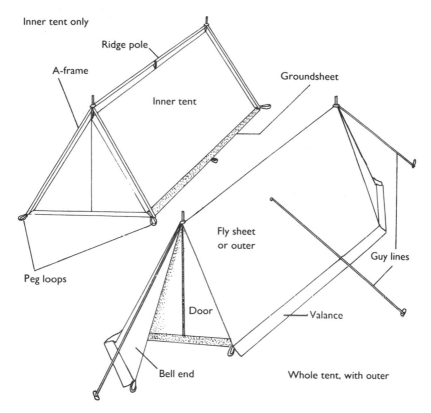

Inner tent only

Ridge pole

A-frame

Groundsheet

Inner tent

Fly sheet
or outer

Guy lines

Peg loops

Door

Valance

Bell end

Whole tent, with outer

**3.1** A traditional A-frame ridge tent.

made with a tent is to reduce the quality of the groundsheet but watch out for this, as keeping the rain out from above is useless if it comes in from below. The inner also usually has a 'no-see-'em' or mosquito net door, in addition to the main one, and you would be foolish to buy a tent without one!

The gap between the inner and outer layers is important: the two must not touch because this would quickly lead to the entry of damp. In modern tents this gap remains small because the two sheets are kept very taut. With older-style tents the gap is larger.

## Which layer first?

No matter what the design, all layered tents will be erected either inner or outer sheet first. Some makers may claim that the two

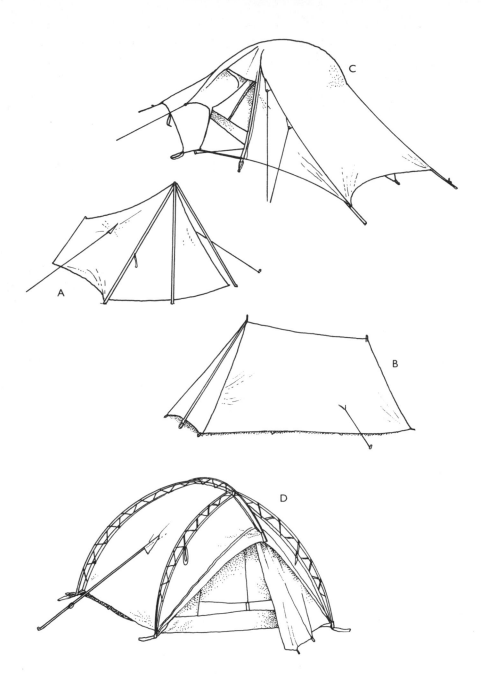

**3.2** Four variations on the ridge tent. The differences are purely superficial; the essential features remain the same.

are erected together for speed but this only means that the two halves are connected in some way – if separated they will still fit into one of the two categories. Each type has its advantages and disadvantages.

If a tent is erected inner first, it means that the poles are attached to the inner and that the outer is thrown over the poles and inner. This gives a very taut tent and means that the gap between the inner and outer can be smaller, giving more space inside. It also means that the tent will not flap as much in the wind and will therefore be much quieter to sleep in. The major disadvantage is that when putting the tent up or down in the rain the inner, which needs to stay as dry as possible, is exposed to the elements for as long as it takes to put the tent up or take it down. If it is raining, the whole tent needs to be put up or taken down very quickly.

In a tent which is erected outer first, the poles are attached to the outer and the inner is then hung from this. The inner is not tensioned and the result is less space, a tent which may flap, and an inner that often sags and looks unpleasant. The major advantage is that, in bad weather, the waterproof outer tent can be put up first and then the inner hung up inside, thus keeping it dry. When taking the tent down it is usually an easy matter to pack up all your gear, take down the inner and put your boots and waterproofs on, all within the comfort of the outer tent.

## Tent design

All modern tents fit loosely into one of four designs: the ridge, the tunnel, the dome or the geodesic. Within these loose categories there are endless variations.

### Ridge tents

Ridge tents are characterized by having poles at either end of the tent. These can be traditional A-poles or a single pole, a variety of flexible poles or a combination of these. A typical combination would be a high A-pole at the entrance, with a short single pole

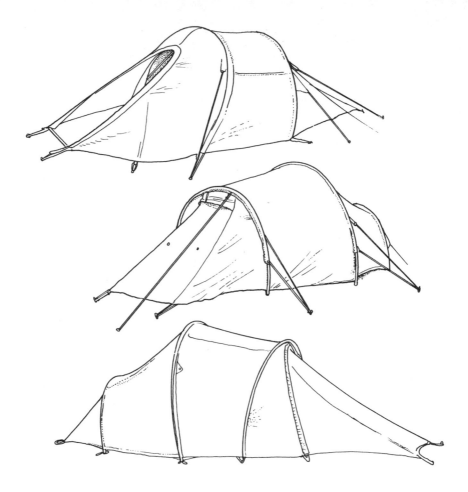

**3.3** Tunnel tents.

at the back end and a sloping ridge (figure 3.2a). This type of tent is often supplied with a choice of A-poles, for convenience, or single poles, for lightness.

Although ridge tents all have a distinct ridge, they do not all have ridge poles. Where they do, these can be either rigid, as in the traditional tent (figures 3.1 and 3.2b) or flexible, as in the modern tent shown in figures 3.2c and 3.2d. These flexible ridge pole tents are often referred to as hoop tents.

Hoop tents are not very strong and need careful erection and

**3.4** Dome tents.

tensioning; they must not be side-on to the wind. Their big advantage is that they are very lightweight and although the inner tents can be quite small the bells (porch areas) are at the side, which makes them very convenient to use. This type of tent is very popular for events such as mountain marathons.

**Tunnel tents**

Tunnel tents were the first development from the traditional A-frame ridge tent. The tent is supported by two or three hoops

45

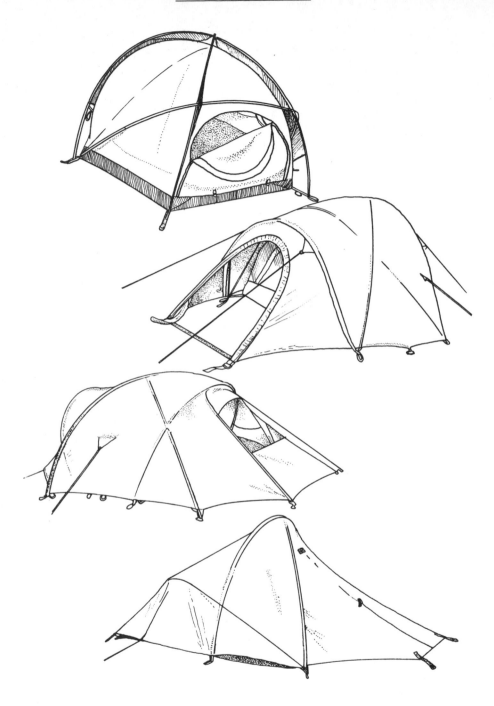

**3.5** Geodesic tents.

running across the tent. These hoops may vary in size, allowing for head room at the front and tapering at the back. This is a popular design for lightweight tents but they can be pushed flat by a strong sideways wind and so need careful erecting.

## Dome tents

Dome tents are based on the traditional igloo design and can have any number of poles crossing at the centre. They make good base camp or valley tents as they give lots of internal room, but they do not perform well in bad weather. Note that any bell area has to be added to the tent as an extra design feature.

## Geodesic tents

This design of tent takes the best features of the tunnel and dome tents, giving a tunnel shape with crossing poles. The tents are very strong and roomy, and they often have sizeable bells at both ends. They will withstand a wind from any direction and will also stand unsupported or pegged, which means that they are suitable for hard or rocky ground. Because of the inherent strength of the geodesic design, manufacturers tend to make this type of tent from stronger, heavier materials for serious mountain use. In addition, they are often fitted with a snow valance and extra guy lines to cope with extreme conditions. These factors, combined with the large number of poles they use, mean that geodesic tents are often heavier than other designs, but versions in lighter materials are becoming available.

## Single-skin tents

Single skin tents are usually made of Gore-tex fabric. Although very light, they do not function as well as a conventional double-skin tent under certain conditions. They are improving all the time, however, and might be worth investigating if you have the money – they are more expensive.

## *Making a choice*

If I was put on the spot and asked which tent to choose, I would go for a geodesic for all-round use and a hoop tent for occasions when I wanted a very light tent that was not going to have to stand up to too much punishment. Your choice should be based on strength, weight, intended use, design features and, in the final analysis, cost.

### Strength

How strong do you need it? If strength is a high priority, the A-frame design with its stronger poles has much to recommend it.

### Weight

Weight will often be your overriding consideration – either you need a very lightweight tent or you do not. In general, if the tent is to be for two or more people then weight becomes less of a consideration. Be aware, however, that design features such as bell space and strength are often sacrificed for weight.

### Intended use

Tents usually have a rating indicating their use ranging from meadow to expedition tents. This is not only a factor of strength but also includes design features such as guy lines, number of pegs needed, height, slope of the top, valance, etc. Do not be tempted to go for a tent that greatly exceeds your needs; you will pay for it in both cost and weight. Many tents which are designed for high mountain use suffer from condensation problems that make them unsuitable for valley use.

### Design features

These include storage/cooking space; number of entrances; ease and speed of erection; internal space and head room; mosquito net doors; colour, etc.

## Cost

There is some truth in the adage that you get what you pay for but beware of paying large amounts of money for 'gimmicks' such as drying lines or fitted pockets. Whilst these may be important, they should not influence the final choice.

## *Care and use of the tent*

Despite the strength of modern tents, they still need a degree of looking after and care. They should never be stored wet but should always be shaken out and hung up to air after every use.

When carrying tents, ensure that they will not get caught or torn: have them inside your rucksack, if possible. In general there is no need to carry the bags that tents are supplied with. If the tent does get torn, manufacturers usually supply patches which can be glued on with any suitable adhesive. If the repair is in a strategic place or is a large one, the edges should be sealed with a seam sealant.

The obvious place to carry the poles is on the outside of the sack but be careful of this. Modern lightweight flexible poles are not very strong and could be easily snapped. When erecting a tent with lightweight poles, be careful not to bend them more than absolutely essential. Broken poles can usually be repaired on a temporary basis with sleeves provided by the makers.

### Erecting the tent

It is always important that you read the manufacturer's instructions and practise with a new tent before you take it out for the first time.

When erecting the tent, check the ground for anything that might damage the groundsheet. Always try and erect the tent with its back into the wind. Pegs are usually designed to be driven in up to the hilt at about 45 degrees; use skewer types for the inner and outer tents and heavier ones for the guy lines.

As a general rule, if a tent looks good with no ripples on the fly sheet and the poles up symmetrically when erected, then it is

| Property | Artificial | Natural |
|---|---|---|
| When wet | Retains its warmth | Is useless and takes a long time to dry |
| Packing size (compressibility) | Is often very bulky although modern bags are getting better | Can pack down into a very small size |
| Weight | Tends to be heavy | Can be very light |
| Warmth | Depends on the bag | Usually very warm |
| Cold spots | Should not happen | Can happen where knees and hips press against cheaper bags |
| Cost | Can often be bought quite cheaply | A good bag will be very expensive |

**3.6** A comparison of the properties of artificial and natural fillings for sleeping bags.

correct. If it looks loose or there are odd pieces flapping, there is something wrong.

## Sleeping bags

When you first look at sleeping bags you might wonder how on earth you are going to know which is the right one for you. The choice is much simpler than you might think and in reality you don't need to understand any of the great mass of figures that will be thrown at you.

### Fillings and ratings

The first choice to make is which filling you want. This is between an artificial filling, usually of 'Hollofil' or something similar, and a natural filling, which will be a combination of down and feathers. The difference between the two is set out in figure 3.6. I tend to use a down bag because it can be compressed so much smaller and weighs less. However, I do take great care that it does not get wet.

Cost is usually a good guide to buying a sleeping bag: if it is cheap and cheerful there is usually a reason. Many bags will be rated by their seasonal use on a scale of one to five seasons, where a one-season rating is for summer lowland use and a five-season rating is for use in the mountains. The top bags are often referred to as expedition bags.

## Construction

You should know a little bit about the construction of sleeping bags. This should not be of the 'sewn-through' type, which would lead to cold spots. Look for a bag which is made in separate compartments, or 'boxes', as this will not only stop cold spots but also prevent the filling from moving around.

## Other features

Do you want a zip? My personal answer would always be yes, as it makes getting in and out of the bag so much easier in the confines of a tent. The zip should always have a baffle along the inside of it to protect you from draughts.

Never buy a bag without a substantial hood and always look for one which has a good shoulder baffle along the top edge to stop draughts coming at the neck.

## Sleeping mats

Until recently there was little choice of sleeping mats; they were all made of closed cellular foam of differing weights. The only option was whether to go for a full-length mat and comfort or a shorter length to save weight. This has all changed recently with the advent of self-inflating mats, notably the 'Therma-rest'. They might seem expensive but once you have spent a few nights using a Therma-rest you will agree that it is worth every penny. The only drawback is that you do have to careful to avoid puncturing these mats.

# Camp-sites

## *Choosing a camp-site*

You cannot always camp wherever you please. It is your responsibility to check the local camping rules and conventions from places such as tourist offices, national park departments and guide books. Once you know that camping is permissible, you can get down to the practicalities of choosing the best site.

The keys to the choice of camp-site are wind and water. You need to avoid both, not only at the time when you arrive but also in anticipation in case a storm should blow in during the night.

---

### Factors to look for:

---

- A site out of the wind, in the lee of hills, woods etc. Be aware that the direction of the wind at the time of your arrival might not be the prevalent one. Think about what would happen to the wind in a storm: will it be funnelled and swirled over a nearby cliff or swirled around a valley? Some wind traps such as high passes are obvious but others can only be spotted with considerable experience or local knowledge.

- A site that will not get flooded. Obviously you need a water supply but watch for streams and rivers which might rise dramatically during the night. Beware also of dips in the ground, which often fill with water during heavy rain, and look out for water run-offs in the hills which might funnel a stream into your site.

- Inherent dangers which might affect the site such as overhanging loose branches, dry-stone walls in bad repair or scree (tallus) slopes.

Do not forget cattle which might be tempted to join you in your sheltered site!

- For comfort, a site which is as flat as possible and free of stones and tree roots. Ten minutes work on arrival will save a long sleepless night.

You might think this is all rather obvious but in my time I have woken up to find that a nearby stream has risen and is flowing through my tent, or that the comfortable dip I pitched my tent in has filled with rain-water. My tent has been flattened by cows and more than once I have spent all night looking for some small pebble digging in my back. Every walker and mountaineer has made at least one of these mistakes.

## Organizing the camp-site

When arriving at your camp-site for the night it is a mistake, but a very forgivable one, to collapse in a big soggy heap and do nothing. Try to stay motivated at least until the tents are up and the stoves lit, then you can collapse. There can be few things more unpleasant than trying to organize a camp-site in the dark and rain, so always assume that it will soon be dark – get your tents up!

If you are in a group the tasks can be split: the tents put up, stoves lit, water collected and, if necessary, firewood collected and a latrine dug.

## Organizing the tent

Tent organization is simply a question of applying the same principles to your tent as to your camp-site. Try to keep your tent tidy and know where things are so you do not have to pull everything out to find them. Be careful to avoid bringing water into the tent via your boots and waterproofs: keep them in the bell end of the tent. Little things, like having a torch and pair of shoes handy during the night and having the stove set up so that in the morning you can just reach over and put a brew on without get-ting up, make a world of difference.

Living in a tent in bad weather takes a fair degree of organization and self-discipline. As you enter the tent, take your boots and water-proofs off in the bell and stow them there. Either get into your sleeping bag or stow it at the end of the tent where it will not get wet. Always keep a set of dry clothes for night use and change into them when you get into the tent. Clothes that are damp rather than wet can be dried by putting them in the bottom of your sleeping bag, but personally I would rather have a good night's sleep – putting on damp clothes in the morning is the lesser hardship.

Once the tents are up, you need to think about water sources (which should be well upstream from your camp-site) and where the latrines will be. The latter need to be away from watercourses and away from the camp-site. Toilet paper should be burnt and the latrine hole should be filled in and covered with turf before you leave.

It is important to exercise some discipline in any camp site. Keep kit stored away and the area clean and tidy – the alternative is that things will soon start to go missing or get wet and the ensuing chaos will spoil what should be a magic experience. Food stocks, left-over food and rubbish need to be stowed away otherwise you will be amazed how much wildlife such as rats and foxes will appear out of a barren landscape and make its way into your camp site after your scraps. In bear and racoon country food should not be left in your tents but placed up a tree away from your site, unless you want to share your sleeping bag with the local shaggy monster!

## Respecting the environment

There is never any excuse for leaving litter in any form. The only acceptable way to dispose of litter is to take *all* of it away with you even if it is biodegradable. It should not be burnt, buried or stuffed under the nearest convenient rock.

Environmental considerations are still, sadly, often a matter of lip service in the UK, although the situation is improving all the time. Faeces, toilet paper and a remarkable amount of litter are still found under walls and rocks in popular camp-sites and by the side of trails. Often there is a token attempt to hide litter by shoving the whole lot into a dry-stone wall or under a rock but this is simply not acceptable. The situation in continental Europe can be even worse and many of the popular camp-sites, even in the wild, become dumps of rubbish and human waste.

There is a lot to be learnt from the tight control exercised in the USA and New Zealand, where popular areas are monitored and subject to controls. Everyone knows what is expected of them. 'Regulations' about camping, toilets and washing being 60m (200ft) from a watercourse, for example, make a lot of sense. In some areas, such as the Grand Canyon and popular trails in New Zealand, rafting and trekking parties are required to bring out with them all waste matter, including rubbish and human excrement.

## Alternatives to camping

Although I have defined backpacking as carrying 'your home on your back', this does not mean that you are compelled to camp. There are several alternatives which provide you with shelter and also enable you to meet other people in a social setting. On a long trip I will often have a night in a hostel after every three or four nights of camping as this gives me a chance to dry my clothes, have a shower and generally sort myself out.

### *Youth hostels*

Traditionally, youth hostels have provided cheap and simple accommodation for walkers, climbers and skiers. In general these hostels, which are not exclusively for young people, are relatively cheap, clean and well run. There are often, various 'rules' to be observed which may include a lights-out time and the obligation to perform a variety of 'chores'.

**3.7** Symbol of the International
Youth Hostel Federation.

# HOSTELLING
# INTERNATIONAL

Most youth hostels are members of the International Youth Hostel Federation (IYHF). There are at present perhaps 5000 hostels in over 60 countries from Algeria to Uruguay and from Germany to Peru. Although each country has its own organization, membership of your national organization gives you access to every other country's hostels as well. The international hostel network is covered by the two-volume International Youth Hostels Guide to Budget Accommodation, which is available from your national organization. You can also use the International Booking Network to book ahead, even for hostels in other countries.

In addition to the IYHF youth hostels there are increasing numbers of independent hostel groups which provide simple accommodation. These hostels are preferred by some people because they are less formal (for example: they do not have times for 'lights out' or 'doors closed'). On the other hand, one of the very things that I like about IYHF hostels is knowing it will be possible to have an uninterrupted night's sleep after a certain time. Independent hostels also vary greatly in standards and facilities, though they are usually cheap!

Contact addresses for many main hostelling organizations are given in the Appendix.

## Lodges

Many countries, notably in trekking areas such as Nepal, India and Thailand, have lodges which are small, very cheap hotels run by local people. They are very basic but they are a great way of meeting people. Smarter versions are the official lodges run by authorities such as National Parks in many countries.

## Private homes

It is possible to stay in people's private homes through an international but little-known organization called Servas, which runs a network of 'hosts' throughout the world. Accommodation is provided free, as the purpose of the visits is cultural exchange. It should be possible to find the address of your nearest Servas organization through the telephone enquiry system. Many countries still have a tradition of welcoming people into their homes, though sadly this is often abused. If you ever get the chance to stay in someone else's home, please treat it with respect and not as a free hotel.

## Bed-and-Breakfast

Bed-and-breakfast accommodation varies greatly from the motels of America to the *gîtes d'étapes* of France and the housewife making a few pounds on the side in Britain. Some, like the European *gîtes*, are run by organizations in a similar way to youth hostels and the guide books to the region will give you the details.

## Mountain huts

Mountain huts range from the huge, crowded and expensive affairs of the French Alps to the bothies of Scotland which are almost a local secret.

Unlocked huts will usually be free and be no more than a shelter containing bunk beds. It is important that you respect such huts. Some will have caches of food, fuel and first aid equipment but these are for genuine emergencies; they are not there just in case you get a bit short.

Other, larger huts might have wardens, who often provide meals. In popular areas they can be expensive and they will always be busy during the climbing season. Off-season, most of these huts will be closed but a single room (usually the basement) is often left open for emergency use. Membership of a mountaineering club which has reciprocal hut rights usually gives a substantial discount at these huts.

Finally there are climbing club huts which are exclusively for club members. Breaking into these huts for a free night's sleep is one of the ultimate crimes in the mountains.

## Bivvy bags

If you have a bit of imagination and knowledge, there is no need to take any of the above options or to carry a tent. When working at Outward Bound Sabah in Malaysia, I was amazed when my students built elaborate shelters every night using nothing more than machetes and poles and bamboo growing in the jungle. Whilst I am not suggesting that you go this far, modern bivvy (bivouac) bags can make a good ultra-lightweight alternative to a tent.

A bivvy bag, usually made of Gore-tex (a layer of microporous material bonded to another material), is in effect a large sleeping-bag cover which you climb into and zip up. If you are claustrophobic, this type of shelter is not for you! Its other disadvantages can be considerable: the lack of space can make getting into your sleeping bag and changing your clothes a real contortion act; and of course cooking has to be done outside. Shelter from the wind will add greatly to your comfort when using a bivvy bag.

Despite the disadvantages, I often use my bivvy bag simply because of its simplicity and extreme lightness.

## Snow shelters

Spending a night in a snow shelter is something that everybody ought to try at least once. The peace, calm and relative warmth

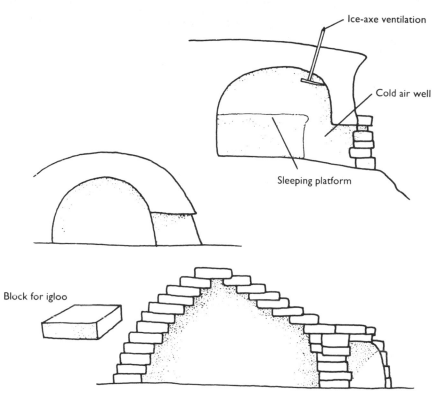

Ice-axe ventilation

Cold air well

Sleeping platform

Block for igloo

**3.8** A typical snow hole.

inside one, even when a storm is blowing outside, has to be experienced to be believed. There are countless different designs but the principles are all the same. A substantial amount of firm snow will be required.

A good building method is to dig an entrance of reasonable size and then expand the shelter from the inside. The entrance can subsequently be blocked up with snow blocks. It is absolutely essential to provide adequate ventilation, however, and if the entrance is too small then ski poles or something similar should be poked through the roof to provide air holes. The hole should also be well marked so that nobody inadvertently walks through the roof.

The *Outward Bound Walker's Handbook* describes snow shelters in greater detail.

# 4

# Food and cooking

## Stoves

The choice of stove depends on many factors, including what type of fuel you prefer and whether it will be available locally.

### Camping stove fuel

The choice of fuel is at best a personal one and at worst a difficult one. All fuels have their own characteristics which make them suitable for different uses. For example: for many years I have used the Trangia type of methylated spirit burning stove for its pure simplicity. However, when travelling through Asia I wanted a stove which would use a variety of fuels and I changed to a Peak One multi-fuel stove. This was wonderful with Coleman fuel but I found it to be rather too volatile when using paraffin. Although I have gone back to a Trangia, my inclinations now are to go to a more powerful stove for winter use, perhaps buying the gas adapter kit which Trangia supplies. In general though, because I work in centres, meths is very easy to come by and that makes this type of stove the natural choice.

---

### The main features of each fuel are:

---

- **Coleman fuel** gives a good powerful flame which in many stoves can be easily controlled; the fuel evaporates quickly and leaves no lingering smell. The disadvantages are that it can be hard to obtain, it is expensive compared with most fuels, the flame can flare when lighting and it can be quite volatile on occasions.

- **Petrol**, although widely available, can be hard to buy in small quantities as well as being rather variable in quality. It does burn well but has the major disadvantage of clogging stoves up very quickly, which means that a lot of maintenance is required.

- **Paraffin** has the advantage of being one of the most widely available fuels in the world, making it ideal for trips to 'exotic' countries. However, it is often polluted in Third World countries and requires straining. Although it does burn well, it is rather volatile and is prone to flaring; it also needs a separate priming fuel to light it.

- **Methylated spirits** is probably the simplest, safest and quietest of the liquid fuels to use; it is also widely available in most countries. Its disadvantage is that it does not give a roaring flame, making it very slow for winter use, and the amount of fuel needed for a long trip makes it a heavy option.

- **Camping Gaz** (Bleuet) was the standard camping stove for many years, and for many families it still is. It is very safe and simple to use and the gas cylinders are widely available. However, it suffers from a number of disadvantages which preclude it from most backpacking trips. The main problem is that a large number of cylinders need to be carried, both in and out; all too often I see discarded fuel cylinders on the hillside. The cylinders give progressively less heat as the fuel level goes down and there is often a residue of fuel left over which can be dangerous if you are not aware of it. Finally, Camping Gaz will not work in very cold temperatures or windy conditions.

- **EPI gas** has many of the advantages of Camping Gaz although it is not as widely available. Besides burning better than Camping Gaz, the main advantage of EPI gas is that the cylinders are self sealing. This means that they can be removed for carrying purposes, and when the fuel level gets low, instead of having to wait for them to be empty as with the Camping Gaz cylinder.

- **Solid/jelly fuels** are available in several varieties and are useful for very lightweight backpacking, such as in mountain marathons or for use as an emergency stove. They are not very efficient and give a low, uncontrollable heat output.

Each fuel has its own inherent dangers, in addition to the obvious hazards of an open flame. Meths burns with a very low flame and it is most important to check that it has actually burnt out before refuelling the stove. Gas cylinders should never be changed near an open flame as they usually leak fuel when unscrewed. The other liquid fuels can be volatile when lighting so need to be kept away from tents, etc.

Most fuels are available in most countries, though some are easier, or harder to find than others. Paraffin, for example, is fairly universal whereas Coleman fuel can be impossible to find in many Third World countries. When travelling abroad, therefore, the choice of stove is often limited by the local fuel available. Guides such as the *Lonely Planet* usually give a good indication of what you can expect.

Figure 4.1 gives a selection of the names by which different fuels are known. Countries not mentioned will use one of these names.

## Choosing a stove

The actual stove you use is a very personal choice. Once you have decided which fuel you deem to be the most suitable, ask yourself a few questions.

---
### Questions in choosing a stove:
---

- Do you need a powerful stove?

- Are you going to want to control the flame, for example, for simmering?

- How much weight (of stove and fuel) can you afford to carry?

- Is it important for the stove to have simple maintenance needs?

| COUNTRY | FUEL NAME | | | |
|---|---|---|---|---|
| UK | Paraffin | Unleaded petrol | Coleman fuel | Methylated spirit 'Meths' |
| France | Petrol | Essence sans plomb | Petrol à brûler Essence filtrée Blanche sans plomb | Alcool à brûler Alcool denature Alcool methyique |
| Holland | Petroleum Lampen-olie | Benzine Normaal 16 | | Spiritus Braand Spiritus |
| Germany | Petroleum Paraffinol | Benzine | | Spiritus Brennspiritus |
| Italy | Olio de paraffina | Benzina | | Alcool denaturo Spirito de brucaire |
| Spain | Parafina | Gasolina | | Alcohol metilico |
| Sweden | Fotogen Petroleum | Bensin | Vit Bensin | T-sprit Rod-sprit |
| USA | Kerosene | Gasoline 'Gas' | White gas Naptha Coleman fuel Blazo | Denatured alcohol |

4.1 Names by which different fuels are known.

- What weather conditions (wind and temperature) will the stove be used in?

- Is flaring an issue? For example: will you be cooking in or near your tent a lot?

- Can you readily obtain the fuel?

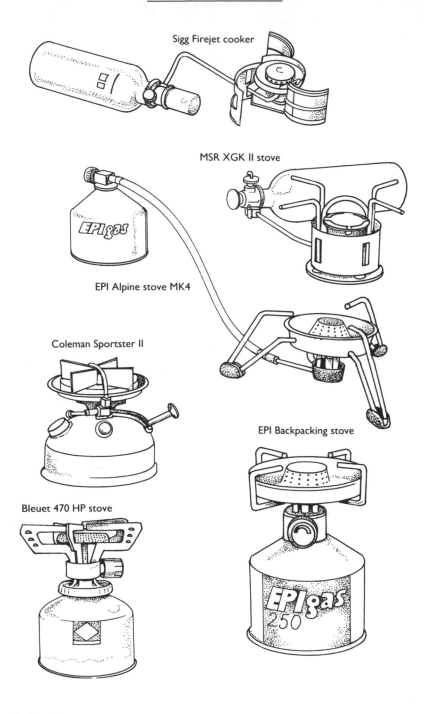

Sigg Firejet cooker

MSR XGK II stove

EPI Alpine stove MK4

Coleman Sportster II

EPI Backpacking stove

Bleuet 470 HP stove

**4.2** Popular stoves.

- Is pre-heating going to be a problem?

- How important is simplicity of use?

- And finally – cost?

The Trangia methylated spirit stove accounts for the great bulk of stoves bought and used by groups in the UK at the moment. It is light and simple, and the stove kit includes all the pots and pans. The main danger with this type of stove is that the fuel burns with an invisible flame in daylight and people have been know to refill a lit burner thinking it has gone out – with disastrous consequences. Always check that the stove is out and cold (use your hand) before you refill it.

## Using the stove

The first consideration when using any stove must be safety. I own a tent with a large hole in the snow valance around the entrance, caused when a previously reliable stove suddenly

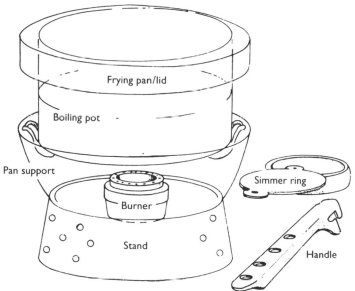

4.3 The Trangia stove: a cross-section.

spurted out burning fuel whilst I was cooking in the bell of the tent. Luckily there was a bucket of water handy with which a prompt camper nearby was able to put out the fire before it really took hold. The lesson is only too clear: stoves are very dangerous.

I am not going to preach the 'never cook in your tent' sermon, at some stage everyone is going to experience weather conditions which leave them no choice but to cook under cover. **Remember that tents can burn to the ground, often in seconds,** and that most modern equipment and clothing have either low burning or low melting temperatures. Another, often neglected, safety aspect is that all stoves use oxygen when alight and so should never be used in a sealed area. For example: a badly ventilated snow hole could be a potential death trap.

---

### When using the stove bear in mind these simple points:

---

- As far as possible, place the stove out of the wind. Stoves vary greatly but, as a general rule, wind is bad!

- Make the stove level and secure. Apart from the obvious safety considerations there is nothing more annoying than dropping your dinner all over the floor just before it comes to the boil.

- Ensure that you have enough fuel for the meal. Running out of fuel half way through cooking is a nightmare – especially if you do not notice for half an hour and sit there wondering why the meal is taking so long!

- When boiling water, cover the pan. This sounds obvious but it can save ages.

- Organize your cooking so that everything is ready at once, rather than having your mashed potato twenty minutes after your stew. Often this is a case of cooking everything and then reheating it all, piling pans on top of each other (if safe to do so) to maximize the use of the heat.

- Do not put hot pans on the ground as the warmth will quickly drain out of them. Be careful about putting them straight on to your groundsheet, which might well melt.

- If you must cook under cover, use the bell of your tent and ideally leave one flap open. Do not leave things like sacks and boots in the bell whilst you are cooking. Be aware of how you will get out if the worst does happen and the tent entrance catches fire. Also be aware of the amount of condensation that can be caused by cooking and ensure the area is well ventilated.

- Let one person do the actual cooking. This might sound odd but camping stoves are not large cooking ranges and too many people fussing over them might mean the dinner ends up on the ground rather than in your stomach, especially if you are cooking in a confined area like the bell of your tent.

- Scrupulously observe simple hygiene rules such as washing your hands, pots and utensils. Stomach bugs have ruined many a good trip.

- And finally – wash up immediately, it will save hours later!

## Food

A great deal has been written about the various fats, proteins and carbohydrates that are needed on expedition, and so I do not intend to cover nutrition in any great detail here. As well as nutritional balance, it is important to take food which you actually enjoy and to take lots of it, within the limits of your carrying capacity.

### Choosing food for a walking and camping trip:

- Buy something that you like and that everyone will eat.

- Choose sensible foods. Junk food simply will not give you enough energy return. Choose food with a high carbohydrate content and more fat than normal; these are the energy suppliers and are usually found in sugar and starches. Dehydrated pasta meals are one of the best choices.

- Keep the weight down. There is really no need to carry cans and bottles these days; not only do they have to be carried in but also the empty containers must be carried out. There is a huge range of easy-to-carry dehydrated food on the market.

- Avoid the specialist camping meals. They cost a fortune and the same things can be found in supermarkets for half the price.

- Keep the meals simple. Try to choose meals which consist of one main dish, such as stews or pasta. Many of these are simple to prepare: add boiling water and leave them to stand or simmer for a few minutes.

- Avoid meals that need simmering or boiling for more than a few minutes, as no one has the patience to cook them correctly. They are also very expensive in terms of fuel.

- Take more than you think you will need. Packets which say 'a meal for two or three' will usually be enough for only one hungry walker. You expend huge amounts of energy when out walking and it needs to be replaced.

- Take plenty to drink – any liquid except alcohol. You need to drink far more than you might expect. For example, if you normally drink three cups of tea a day at home, you will be drinking six or seven when out on the hill. Walking is thirsty work and also you must maintain your fluid levels to avoid dehydration. This applies no matter what the weather. Even when you are cold you can lose a lot of fluid. Drinks can also be very warming and a major morale booster.

- Plan ahead. You should have an exact menu so that you are not carrying surplus food or, even worse, not enough.

## Breakfast

Many people still cook eggs and bacon when out walking, but for most people it is simply too much hassle and the pans are always a nightmare to wash afterwards. Personally I go for small ready-made packets of muesli which have milk powder in them so I only need to add water, this is followed by a couple of bread rolls, or biscuits on a longer trip, with jam. If you can get hold of the small catering packs they are perfect for this. Forget about toast: it is not possible to toast bread over the average backpacking stove.

I always ensure that the kettle is filled last thing at night and that the stove is within reach of the tent door so that I can have my first cup of tea whilst still in my sleeping bag – absolutely essential!

## Lunch

Lunch should be kept as simple as possible. If anything, 'little and often' is a better technique than stopping for a long lunch break, unless it is a particularly nice day. Go for things like biscuits, or rolls, and cheese or various spreads; the types found in tubes are best. Chocolate bars are a good source of energy.

Many people advocate taking a stove for the lunchtime brew. Personally I prefer to make up a flask of hot tea in the morning so that it is ready whenever I need a drink.

When you stop for lunch (indeed whenever you stop for any time) ensure that you are sheltered from the elements, including the sun or the wind. If it is cold, you should also put on extra layers of clothing when you stop, though this might be the last thing you want to do if you are all hot and sweaty from slogging up a hill. You will, however, cool down dramatically in no time.

## Evening meal

This is the meal that matters; if nothing else, it sets you up for a comfortable night in your tent. Generally, as soon as I reach my camp-site, the stove goes on for the first brew and then I put up my tent and get sorted whilst the water is boiling. Make the evening meal as civilized as you can, go for three courses and enjoy it.

Packet soup is a good way to start; drink it from your mug so that the pan can be used to boil the water for the next course. Make absolutely sure that any dehydrated food is well cooked; if it is not, it will taste awful and continue to rehydrate in your stomach, giving you stomach ache through the night. I usually try to finish with something sweet like tinned fruit, which will often be the only tin I carry, but of course fresh fruit is just as good.

The secret of an efficient evening meal is to keep the stove constantly on the go. Whilst eating one course the next course should be on the stove, and when eating the last course the water should be boiling for a final brew and the washing up.

### The final touch

Although some people might do so, I have never prepared fresh meals whilst backpacking – I believe the weight factor of carrying a variety of ingredients plus the hassle involved does not make it worthwhile. Modern pre-prepared and pre-packed meals are widely available and are usually more than adequate. There are a few exceptions: whilst working at Outward Bound Sabah the pre-prepared meals consisted of nothing but rice and fish – every day!

I do take a few little oddments such as a packet of mixed herbs, some tomato purée or perhaps garlic, as many of the packaged mince meals can be somewhat bland. If I pass a shop I usually buy a few things such as mushrooms or carrots to spice up the meal that evening. In general I find that adding these little extras to the normal packaged meals is the ideal compromise.

There are a few extras which make cooking and camping more pleasurable. I always take a wooden spoon as I hate the thought of a metal spoon scraping the pan. For eating I use a normal spoon and do not bother with a knife and fork (although I always have my trusty Swiss army knife). I carry a large drinking mug as the cups on the top of flasks are often a bit small. You can buy small fold-up can openers from camping shops which, although fiddly, are easy to accommodate.

# 5

# Navigation: the theory

Never think that navigation is only for the experts or that it is an inexplicable art. In fact, it is both simple and fun. There are two halves to navigation: the theory of map and compass work, and the practicality of route-finding when out walking.

---

**The theoretical side of navigation can be split into three elements:**

---

- Direction: which way?
- Distance: how far?
- Visualization: what does it look like?

---

The basic equipment requirements of navigation are a map and a compass. Despite the views held by many beginners, the compass is of secondary use; a knowledge and understanding of the map is the key to navigation.

## The map

A map should be regarded as simply a bird's-eye view of the ground. Indeed, if you look closely at a map you will see that most of the symbols which seemed complex at first are simply small pictures. Although maps the world over vary greatly in quality and style, there are a number of key areas that are common to them all. The two most important things you need to know initially about a map are its scale (relative size) and its orientation (which way up it is).

## Scale

There is nothing magical about scale, but if the numbers seem too large to cope with, try reducing them to decimal equivalents. For example: a map scale of 1:25000 means that every 'unit' on the map represents 25000 'units' on the ground. If the unit on this map is 1cm, it represents 25000cms on the ground, which is 250m or 0.25km. You have arrived at the simple truth that 1:25000 means that 1cm on the map equals 0.25km on the ground, or 4cm represents 1km. The maths in imperial units does not work out quite as neatly, although the principle is exactly the same: in this case 2.5in on the map represents one mile on the ground.

A map with a scale of 1:50000 is good for general walking but a 1:25000 map, if available, gives much more detail and is of more use in mountainous areas. Imperial-scale maps have traditionally been 1in to the mile (or 1:63360) but this is really starting to get too small for detailed map work.

There is always going to be a compromise between the detail you require and the physical size of the map. A scale of anything larger than 1:25000 would give you an impossibly large map to handle, whereas anything less than 1:50000 would not have enough detail. Orienteering maps, which need a lot of detail but only cover very small areas, are typically about 1:10000. Some maps on the market are 1:40000, which is a good compromise although it does take a little getting used to if you have not used one before.

## Orientating the map

Once you know the scale, you need to know which way up the map should go. The easiest method (assuming you know where you are) is to line up an obvious feature on the ground with its map symbol. This is known as orientating (or setting) the map on the ground.

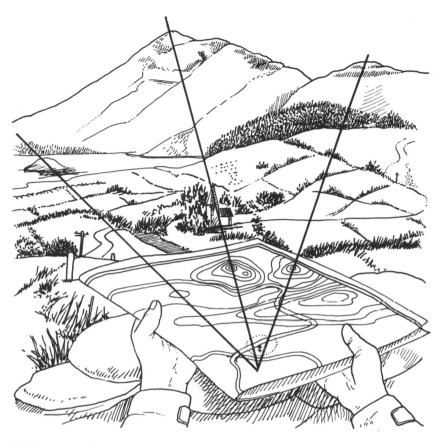

5.1 Orientating the map on the ground.

This method of setting a map is so simple that, assuming you can see the ground, it should become automatic and continuous so that the map is always facing the right way. Do not worry if the writing on the map is not the right way up – it is the direction that counts. The feature could be an obvious single one, such as a high point, or it could be a linear feature such as a river, lakeside or valley.

The second way of setting your map is by using the compass, (figure 5.2). This is done quickly and simply by aligning the rotating north-pointing arrow on your compass (figure 5.9) with the north indicator on your map. Nearly all maps have north at the top edge but check that this is so.

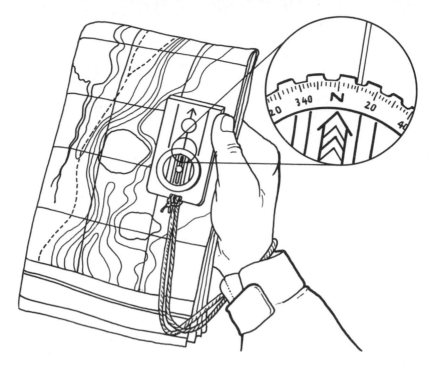

5.2 Setting the map accurately with a compass.

This compass method is perfectly acceptable for keeping the map roughly aligned with north, but there is one complication: maps tend to be aligned with 'grid north' or, occasionally, 'true north'. Your compass aligns itself with 'magnetic north', which is not the same. The difference between these angles is known by a number of terms, the most common of which are 'magnetic variation', 'declination' or 'grid-magnetic angle'. This variation is discussed in detail on p.83.

## Visualization

The key to really understanding a map is to see it as a view of the ground from the air; in other words, to be able to visualize the ground from the map. The three main features on the map which help you to do this are contours, colours and symbols.

## Contours

Almost all maps depict contours, as they are an essential aid to understanding the form of the ground. The colour will vary but they tend to be brownish for the land and blue if under water. Contour lines may seem complex but they are in fact easy to understand. Remember that they are horizontal lines which run at the same height across the ground. If this is hard to visualize, imagine that the sea-level is rising with an incoming tide. When it has risen 10m (33ft), for example, a line is drawn right around what is the new shore. When the sea rises another 10m (33ft), another line is drawn, and so on.

It can be seen from figure 5.3 that, although contours on the map vary in the distance they are apart, the vertical difference is always constant. The slope on the left, for example, is much steeper and so the contours are closer together than they are for the slope on the right. Note also the large gap in the contours where the ground levels off just before the summit. You can see from this example how, with a little practice, you can visualize the

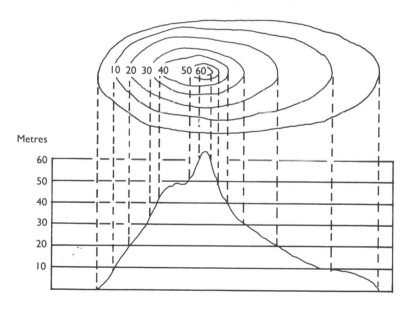

5.3 Contour lines, shown on the ground (in section) and as they would appear on a map (in plan).

shape of the ground from the contours on the map. This is one of the most important skills in map-reading, because the shape of the ground is one of the few things that can usually be relied upon not to change with time. It can be used, therefore, both to work out where you are and to keep track of where you should be.

It is not enough to know the shape of the contours; you also need to know which is up and which is down and what height is involved. In figure 5.4, for example, the contours could represent any of the four land shapes.

If we add a few details to the contours, as in figure 5.5, then it can be seen how the picture changes. In (a) the addition of a stream shows that the contours represent a valley; in (b) the addition of a triangulation point shows that they represent a ridge; whilst in (c) the numbers show that they represent a slope, rising from right to left.

Contours on map

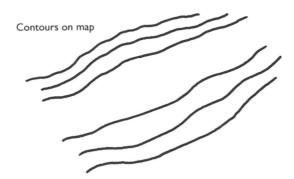

Possible cross-sections on the ground

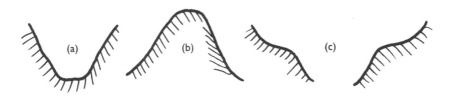

5.4 Contour lines without other details can be misleading. The contours as shown on the map might be interpreted in several different ways in cross-section on the ground.

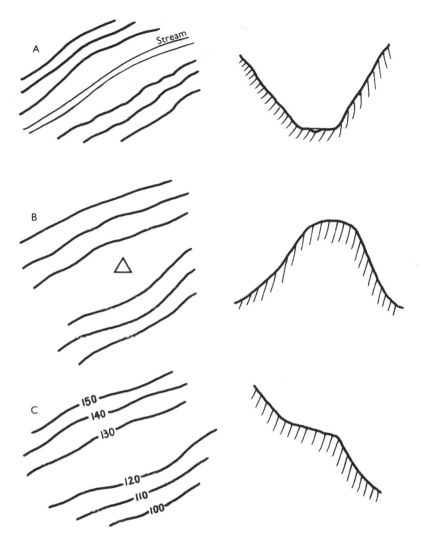

5.5 Contour lines with other details are much clearer: (a) with a stream marked; (b) with a triangulation point; (c) with heights of contour lines.

Numbers, or heights, on contours are usually (but not always) shown facing uphill, in other words if you were looking at the slope the numbers would be the right way up.

We also need to know the 'contour interval', or how far apart the contours are. On the 1:25000 maps the interval is 10m, with every fifth contour shown as slightly thicker to help when counting. The contour interval will be shown somewhere on your map and it is important that you find it so that you visualize how steep slopes are. Note that contours may be left out on very steep ground and that on extremely steep ground they might be omitted altogether and the relevant symbol for crags or cliffs substituted instead.

## Colours and symbols

Colours vary in their exact detail from map to map but there is a general underlying trend which makes them easy to understand. Put simply, the colour on the map tends to reflect the colours on the ground. For example: woods tend to be shown in green whilst rivers are in blue and houses are black. Some maps have shading to show the lie of the ground but this is intended as nothing more than a visual aid.

Symbols are similar to colours in that they tend to show a logical representation of the feature on the ground. Indeed the two together will be found to be even more logical. An example here would be that symbols which look like tufts of grass would represent rough ground if they were brown but boggy ground if blue. Whilst most symbols and colours are logical, it is important that you refer to the legend (or key) on your map and learn at least the most important or most confusing ones.

Perhaps the worst symbols to learn are those showing rights of way and boundaries. It would be a mistake to look for a footpath, for example, when the map symbol is for a village boundary. The best answer is to learn these symbols by rote.

Do not be too quick to cut the legend off your map thinking that it will reduce the amount of paper you are carrying. There will always be a symbol that misleads you.

## *Grid references*

Although the actual information on the grids may change from country to country, the process of reading the reference is always the same. For the examples in this section we have used the

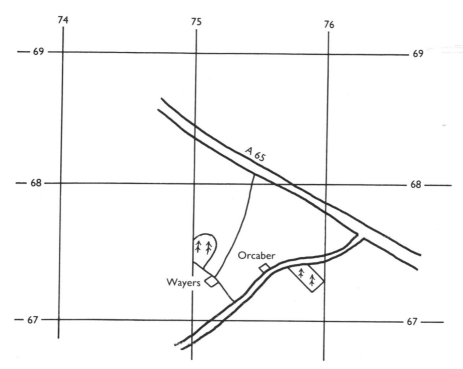

5.6 Reading a grid reference.

Ordnance Survey 1:25000 map, which is the standard map used for hill walking in the UK.

Looking at the example in figure 5.6, if you require a reference for the building known as Orcaber you first need to identify the square in which it lies. To do this, take the numbers that intersect at the bottom lefthand corner of the square: the numbers along the top or bottom of the map first (the easting) and the numbers along the edges of the map (the northing) second. This gives a grid reference for the square of 75 67. This four-figure grid reference is accurate to 1km, (the size of the square).

As this reference could relate to anywhere in the square, you need to reduce it still further. This is done by mentally dividing the square into ten along each edge (figure 5.7).

Again read along the bottom edge first and then the sides. In this case the numbers are 5 and 3, and these numbers are then

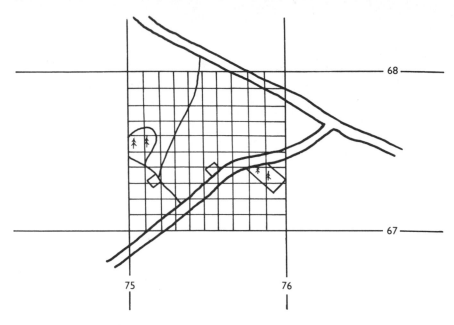

5.7 Subdividing a grid square into ten.

added to the first two pairs, giving 755 673. This six-figure grid reference is accurate to 100m, which should be accurate enough for your purposes. To complete the reference it is possible to add the code letters that are found on the map index, which in this case would give SD 755673. This unique grid reference, if using Ordnance Survey maps, can only refer to Orcaber in the Yorkshire Dales of England. The technique used would be the same for any other series of maps or charts.

**Romers**
Although, with a bit of practice, mentally dividing a square into ten is accurate enough for most purposes, it is both more accurate and quicker to use a Romer as shown in figure 5.8. These can be bought by themselves but can also be found on the baseplates of many compasses. In the example above the four-figure grid square reference is read as before and then the final two figures are read from the Romer scale.

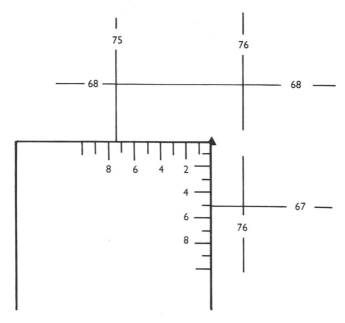

5.8 Using a Romer to pinpoint a grid reference.

## The compass

Although the map and compass are always treated as if they are two halves of an inseparable pair, in reality the compass comes second to good map work. On a good day with reasonable visibility there will rarely be any need for a compass. It is when the visibility is dramatically reduced through bad weather or nightfall that the compass comes into its own, and a compass will be found essential if there are few features on the ground, as in the desert or arctic regions.

Many types of compass are suitable for walking, the one that is simplest to use is a compass that is also a protractor (figure 5.9). This lets you take angles both from the ground (as a compass) and from the map (as a protractor).

It is not essential that a compass should have all of the features shown in figure 5.9. The Romers and magnifying lens, for example, are useful but not vital. This type of compass, often called a

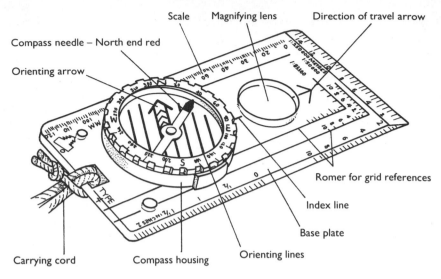

Scale    Magnifying lens    Direction of travel arrow

Compass needle – North end red

Orienting arrow

Romer for grid references

Index line

Base plate

Carrying cord    Compass housing    Orienting lines

5.9 The compass.

baseplate or protractor compass, has a clear plastic base, usually with a ruler on one or more sides, a direction-of-travel arrow at one end and a circular housing for the compass needle mounted at the other end.

This housing, which carries the magnetic needle, rotates in relation to the baseplate. Around the edge of the housing is marked the direction, or bearing, usually in degrees, and this is read off against the index mark on the baseplate. At the bottom of the compass housing are marked a number of index lines and a north arrow, whilst the magnetic-north needle will be coloured at one end to show which is its north end.

## Orientating the map with the compass

We have already covered setting the map quickly by aligning the magnetic-north needle with the top of the map (see page 73). If there is a magnetic variation to be applied this is simply done by setting the variation on the compass housing against the index mark on the baseplate, align the edge of the baseplate with the grid lines on the map and then turn both map and compass together until the magnetic-north arrow lies over the north arrow in the bottom of the compass housing.

## Magnetic variation

This angle, which I shall simply call variation, varies from a few degrees in the UK to 20 degrees or more in western USA. The variation can also be east or west of your map north. The *Outward Bound Map and Compass Handbook* gives a very full and detailed description of how to understand, work out and apply the angle of variation. Here I shall merely say that you need to find out what it is and in which direction to apply it. If the variation is west, the maxim 'mag to grid get rid, grid to mag add' has served many of us well for many, many years. The angle itself is usually found somewhere on the margin of your map, hopefully with a diagram of whether it is is east or west.

If the angle of magnetic north is given as west of the map north, then the variation is added when taking angles from the map and applying them to a compass, and subtracted when taking angles from a compass and applying them to a map. The opposite applies if the angle is given as east.

An added complication is that the angle varies from year to

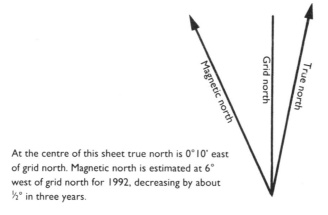

At the centre of this sheet true north is 0° 10' east of grid north. Magnetic north is estimated at 6° west of grid north for 1992, decreasing by about ½° in three years.

5.10 A typical diagram showing magnetic variation. Note that, although true north is referred to, in this case the map is aligned to grid north and so true north becomes irrelevant.

year, for reasons which are not fully understood. Somewhere on your map there should be details of this change and how to apply it. In extreme examples, such as the north of Norway, there may be a large difference in the variation from one side of the map to the other. If this happens, you need to keep your wits about you!

For setting the map with the compass, it can be seen that if the magnetic variation is only a degree or two then it can be ignored (you could not hold the map that accurately for long in any case). However, if the variation is a large one then it needs to be applied.

### Reading a bearing from the map

To read a bearing from the map, first align the edge of the base-plate between the points you wish to use. Always ensure that

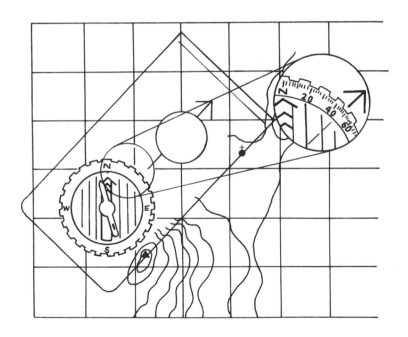

5.11 Reading a bearing from the map.

the direction-of-travel arrow on the baseplate is pointing from the position you want a bearing *from* to the position you want a bearing *to*. Next, rotate the compass housing until the grid lines in the housing are aligned exactly with the grid lines on the map and the north arrow in the housing is pointing to north on the map. Read the number which is next to the index mark on the baseplate.

This number (49 degrees in the example in figure 5.11) is called a grid bearing. Note that it was taken from the grid lines and that the magnetic arrow was not used in the process. If you now want to convert this bearing to a magnetic bearing for use whilst walking, you would have to apply the magnetic variation. Using the variation in figure 5.10 this would be 6 degrees west in 1992, decreasing by half a degree in three years. As the baseplate compass can only be realistically read to 1 degree, this can be left as 6 degrees which means that the magnetic bearing in this example becomes 49 plus 6, or '55 degrees magnetic'. When writing down bearings, always stipulate whether they are magnetic or grid.

If the distance between your two points is greater than the length of the base plate, you have to improvise with a ruler or similar straight edge to extend the scale.

## Reading a bearing from the ground

To read a bearing from the ground, it is first necessary to line up the direction-of-travel arrow with the feature on the ground to which you wish to take a bearing. This needs to be done as accurately as possible, which does take a bit of practice. The compass housing is then turned until the north arrow in the housing matches the magnetic north arrow. The bearing (316 degrees in the example in figure 5.12) is then read from the housing next to the index mark.

This is a magnetic bearing and is fine for walking on. If you wish to plot it on the map, then you will need to subtract the magnetic variation.

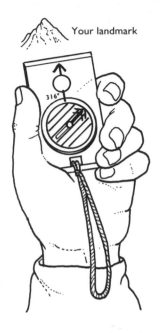

Your landmark

To take a bearing on a landmark, point the direction-of-travel arrow at the landmark and place the north end of the needle in the north end of the gate. Read the bearing at the index mark.

5.12 Reading a bearing from the ground.

## *Walking on a bearing*

Once you have worked out your bearing (and remember it must be a magnetic bearing to walk on), you need to know how to use it. Putting it very simply, keep the bearing on the housing set against the index mark on the base plate, turn the whole compass until the magnetic north arrow matches the housing north arrow and then walk in the direction of the direction-of-travel arrow.

In reality it is not this simple: holding the compass and trying to walk in the direction of the arrow is almost impossible. A better technique is to look along the direction-of-travel arrow and pick out an obvious feature on the ground, walk to that and then repeat the process. If there is no visible feature (because of mist, for example) then substitute a member of your group. Get someone to walk out in front of you in the correct direction. When they stop, get them to move left or right until they are in exactly the same direction as the direction-of-travel arrow and then walk

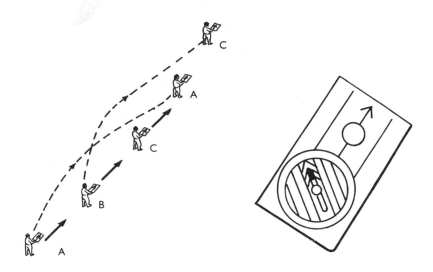

5.13 Leap-frogging a group on a compass bearing. A directs B and then moves to the front; B directs C and then moves to the front; C directs A, etc.

to them. A good group can do this by leap-frogging (figure 5.13) so that as one person is putting the person or feature in the right position with the compass, other group members are already walking forwards. The person who has just been put into position then puts the next person on the bearing whilst the person who was last using the compass is walking to the front of the group.

# 6

# Route-finding in practice

The essence of route-finding, the second half of navigation, can be encapsulated in the maxim: 'You cannot get lost if you always know where you are.'

Once you have practised the theory of map and compass work, it is time to get outdoors and put it into use. The secret here is keep it simple. There is nothing complicated about navigation – it is just a question of keeping your 'legs', or stages, short and using a bit of common sense.

## Navigation by features

In the example in figure 6.1 it would be possible to start at 'A', take a bearing to 'B' from the map, convert it to a magnetic

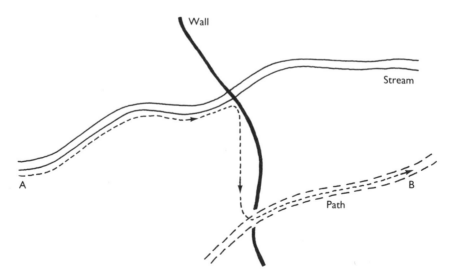

6.1 Using features as aids to navigation.

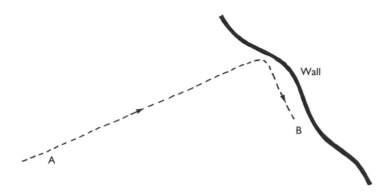

6.2 'Aiming off' to a linear feature.

bearing, measure the distance from the map, using the map scale, and then use these to walk straight to point 'B'. But why bother if using the natural features as 'handrails' means that you are not going to get lost and you can enjoy the walk rather than worrying about navigation? It is a little more complicated if 'A' or 'B' are not on obvious linear features such as walls or tracks, but not greatly so.

## Aiming off

In the example in figure 6.2 'A' is not on a feature. It would be possible to walk straight to 'B' but this would not be advisable: if you were to miss point 'B', you would not know which way to turn at the wall to reach it. This problem can be avoided by 'aiming off'. This means that if you deliberately head just to the left of 'B' you know that, when you reach the wall, you have to turn right to reach it. Remember that the feature does not have to be something as solid as a wall – something like the top of a ridge would do just as well in the mountains.

## Attack points

If it is 'B' that is not on any feature, the aim should be to reduce

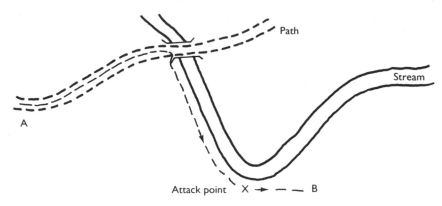

6.3  Using an attack point.

to an absolute minimum the length of the leg where the compass is needed. This is because each fraction of a degree you are out on your bearing will take you away from the point, and the longer the leg the further off you will be.

In figure 6.3 you have navigated from 'A' to the 'attack point' using the path and stream. An attack point is a definite and obvious feature (in this case a distinct bend in the stream) which enables you to take a bearing to 'B' knowing with certainty from where you are taking the bearing.

## Check features

In each of these examples you have used 'check features'. These are anything which can be mentally or physically ticked off as you pass them. Check features are the key to keeping track of where you are on the map.

Another good way of using check features is to have an idea of what lies beyond the point you are trying to find. In the example in figure 6.4 you have left 'A' and aimed off left to the wall, turned right to meet the path, checked off the path/stream junction and the bend in the path and then used the next path/stream junction as your attack point. Your bearing to 'B' was slightly out but this is not a problem because you knew that there was a wall

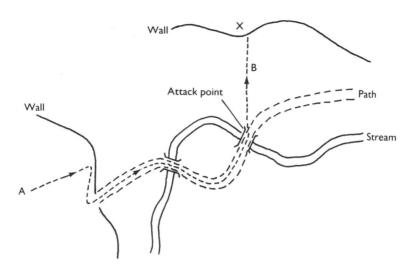

6.4  Using check features to break down a complex leg.

just beyond it, which has checked you from going too far. It is a
simple matter to return to the stream and try again.

Figure 6.4 is a very simple example showing how a complex
leg can be broken down into easy stages and each stage checked
off. It is simple because all the features are very obvious, but in
reality the best check features are natural ones and the best of all
is the slope of the land. This is where good interpretation of contours comes into its own. For example: the final check feature in
figure 6.4 might have been where the angle of the slope started
to steepen rather than something as artificial as a wall.

## Timing and pacing

In addition to knowing the direction you are walking in and having an idea of the land you are passing over, it is important to
know how far you are walking. This knowledge can be used in
two ways: firstly as a direct aid to navigation (in that a distance
combined with a bearing gives you enough information to walk
on) and secondly as a running check on your progress, or in
other words as a movable check feature.

There are two ways to measure the distance you have walked: you can either physically measure the distance or you can calculate the time it will take you to walk that distance. The first is used for shorter legs and involves pacing; the second is used for longer legs and an overall picture and is referred to as timing.

## Timing

Your personal speed will be different from that of someone else. It will also vary with the load you are carrying, the condition of the ground underfoot and, most importantly, the gradient of the ground. There is no hard and fast rule for any of these factors and the only way to discover your speed is to get into the great out-doors and time yourself. However, there are average speeds and these are used in the following examples.

### Flat ground

The easiest timing is a simple walk over flat ground. Unladen, the average speed is approximately 4kph (2.5mph) on the flat, so a walk of 12km (7.5 miles) can be calculated as taking 3 hours. A leg of 500m (0.3 miles) would take about 8 minutes.

If you were to put on a large rucksack, these times would probably drop to about 3kph (1.9mph) or even slower.

### Uphill gradients

Travelling uphill will slow you down again. On average it takes an extra minute for every 10m (33ft) that you climb. This is quite convenient as it means that, on the 1:25 000 map, you can simply add one minute for each contour crossed when going uphill. This extra time is not only because we all slow down when going uphill but also to allow for the foreshortening effect which the bird's-eye-view of the map gives us.

On short legs where the gradient is very gentle and the surface is good, it may be that this extra time is not needed; alternatively, on very steep ground it may be necessary to add more time. This will

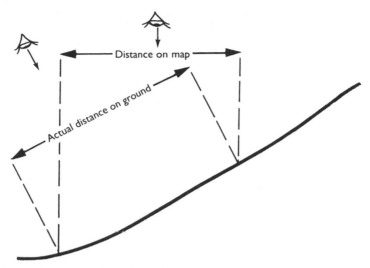

6.5   The foreshortening effect of a gradient.

apply when timing short legs but treat each climb the same when calculating an overall time – the times will balance out.

## Downhill gradients

When travelling downhill on reasonable slopes we tend to walk slightly faster than on the level. However, steep downhill slopes can take quite a bit longer. Again, this will need to be taken into account on short legs but when calculating for the overall walk these times tend to cancel each other out and so downhill legs are not usually compensated for.

## Timing a leg

In the example in figure 6.6, the horizontal distance covered is 3km (1.9 miles) which, with rucksacks on will take 60 minutes. There are two climbs, the first being 50m (165ft) and the second 70m(230ft), which means that 5 and 7 minutes need to be added, giving a total of 72 minutes for the leg. There are a couple of descents but these are ignored. If you had been walking on this leg for 100 minutes, you would start to suspect that you had made a mistake somewhere. You would also know that the top of

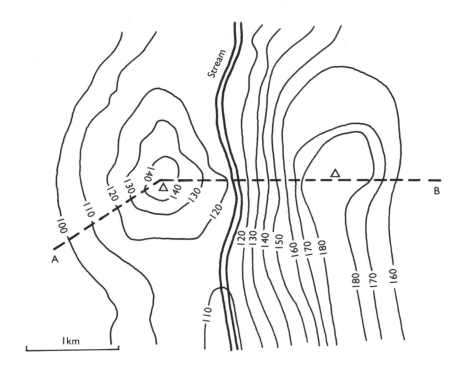

**6.6** An example of timing a leg.

the first climb could not be the objective if it has only taken 25 minutes (1km/0·6mile plus 50m/164ft of climb). Note that each climb is added up separately and the time is for the total height climbed, not just the height of the highest point of the day.

Timing should become second nature to any walker. You should always know not only how long the whole walk will take but also how long each leg will take. It does not have to be accurate to the last minute but it needs to be accurate enough for you to know when you have gone wrong.

## Pacing

Pacing is a much more accurate way of measuring distance. Again everyone will have a different pace and it will also vary with the terrain and the gradient. Realistically, pacing can only be used on short legs as attempting to count more than 500 or so paces would be too cumbersome. Having said that, in extreme conditions (on a featureless plateau in bad visibility, for example) it may be necessary to count paces continuously.

Before you can start pacing you need to measure your pace against a measured, accurate distance on the ground. Choose a distance that can easily be divided, such as 100m (328ft). When counting your paces walk as normally as possible – the normal inclination to take longer paces must be avoided. Do not count every single step but use double paces instead; for example: only count whenever your right foot touches the ground. The total will be the number of double paces you take for that distance on flat, even ground. Ideally, measure your pace on different terrains and gradients, but you will find that the application of different paces will come with experience. You soon find, for example, that when walking up steep slopes you might easily take twice as many paces as on the level.

When pacing a leg, never count to more than one hundred. Keep count of the hundreds separately. (Using pebbles is one popular technique: for every hundred paces transfer a single pebble from one hand into the other.) If the navigation is difficult, it is useful if one person counts paces, another concentrates on keeping the bearing accurate, and a third keeps an eye on the time as an overall check. If there are enough people in the group, several people could count the paces and the average result could be taken as the distance.

## Bad weather and night navigation

There are no additional techniques for navigating in conditions of bad visibility. It is simply a question of practising what you already know and refining it to a higher level.

A technique such as leap-frogging the group on an accurate bearing whilst others keep a close check on the distance (figure 5.13) is a highly accurate way of navigating to an exact point. The disadvantage is that it is time-consuming and hard work.

The real secret to good navigation in bad visibility is to know *exactly* where you are all the time, because it is so much harder to relocate yourself if you go astray. Keep a close check on your timings and your check features. It is also important to avoid long legs, keeping instead to legs of a few hundred metres or just a few minutes so that you reduce the margin for error. Whenever you take a bearing, be sure you know exactly where you are taking it from and do not relax whilst you are walking on it. This method of navigation, usually called micro-nav, has not only saved countless lives when done well but is also extremely exhilarating. To find a small point such as a triangulation pillar in really bad weather is one of the most satisfying experiences in the hills.

## Relocation

At some stage in your walking career you are going to get lost – everyone does. This is nowhere near as bad as it might at first seem; indeed it is usually a question of not knowing exactly where you are rather than being completely lost. The difference might only be a matter of degree but it is a real one.

For example: you might be on a linear feature such as a path or

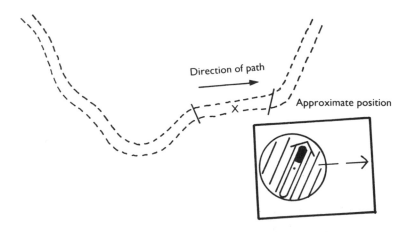

6.7 Using the direction in which a feature is running as an aid to relocation.

a stream but not knowing exactly where on that feature you are. The first step is to see in which direction the feature is running, by taking a bearing along it with your compass. Then by looking at your map you may be able to narrow down where you are by virtue of that direction. It is often as simple as that.

## Backbearings

Failing that, can you make out a distinct feature which you could take a bearing on? If there is, take a bearing on it and add or sub- tract (depending on whether the figure is larger or smaller than 180 degrees) to convert the bearing to a back bearing – in other words the bearing *from* the feature. As this is a magnetic bearing, apply the magnetic variation to convert it to a grid bearing. Place the edge of the compass baseplate on the feature on the map and turn the whole compass until the grid lines in the housing match those on the map. A line along the baseplate edge will now cross your linear feature at the exact spot where you are.

In the example in figure 6.8 you can see a church from the path and you can locate that church on the map. The magnetic bearing to the church is 60 degrees, (a) applying 180 to this gives a back bearing of 240 degrees. Subtracting the magnetic variation of 6 degrees gives a grid bearing of 234 which, when plotted on the map from the church, crosses the path at your location (b).

## Resections

Of course you are not always going to be on an obvious linear feature. In this case if you can see two, or even better three, obvi- ous features which you can find on the map, then you can use a similar backbearing process. This time plot the backbearings from each of your features; your location is where the lines cross. This process (known as resection) is accurate but is rarely used because it is fairly time-consuming. If you can see two or more distinct features you should be able to orientate your map on

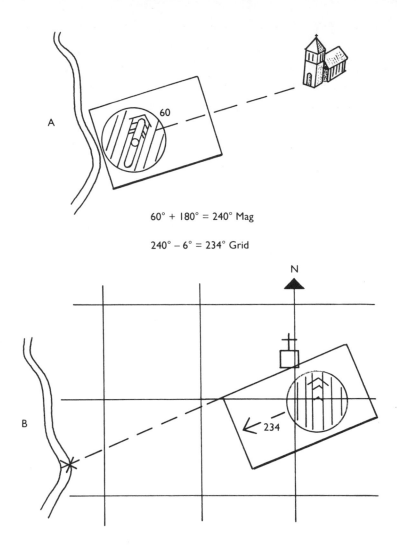

60° + 180° = 240° Mag

240° − 6° = 234° Grid

6.8  Taking a backbearing in order to cross a linear feature.

them to give yourself a rough fix.

## Relocation in poor visibility

To complicate matters further, what happens if you are not on a distinctive feature and the visibility is poor (perhaps the most likely scenario)? First of all sit down and mentally retrace your steps. How long ago did you cross the stream? Has the slope always been going uphill? Once you have done that, check whether there is anything nearby that could help you, in particular in which direction the slope is falling away. If by amassing all these little snippets of information you are still no clearer, then you have to make a choice: do you go on and hope the mist will lift; do you retrace your steps, or do you take some other positive action?

The first choice is the one usually taken and it is also usually the wrong one; it is really a question of 'when in a deep hole – stop digging'. The second option, retracing your steps, will work if you are sure you can head back the way you came, and you do not mind heading backwards!

The third option, although the hardest, is usually the best: this entails effectively abandoning your route until you find where you are. Your aim in this case should be to reach any definite linear feature which you can follow to safety. Firstly, look at your map: is there an obvious long linear feature which you must reach if you walk in a particular general direction – for example, a road which runs along the edge of a mountain range? If there is, set your compass to a suitable direction and walk on that bearing until you reach the feature. Once there you will still have to decide which way to turn but at least you will be on a definite feature.

If there is no one obvious feature, you will have to find any feature which heads downhill and follow it until you come out to somewhere recognizable. A word of warning – beware of following rivers too closely: although they are good features because they always run downhill, they also have a nasty tendency to do so regardless of how steep the ground is. A large waterfall in your way might help your relocation but that would be no consolation if you have already fallen over it!

The important thing is that when you walk anywhere you must keep an eye on your compass, otherwise you will simply wander around aimlessly. You should never rely on instincts or what you feel to be an instinctive feel for the right direction. Our natural sense of direction is poor at the best of times and disappears altogether in poor conditions. To believe otherwise is courting disaster. Nor should you ever rely on your previous knowledge in bad weather and poor visibility. What appears to be instinct in others is usually a good map memory combined with common sense.

## Common-sense checks

Common sense should complement your map and compass skills. Sadly, people have died because they walked 180 degrees in the wrong direction; and we all do it.

The best aid to common sense is the angle of slope: always know whether you should be walking uphill or downhill and whether the slope should be going away on your left or your right. If you get the niggling feeling that it is wrong then stop and check your map. Recently I walked for over an hour with the knowledge at the back of my mind that I should be going steeply downhill when in actual fact I was on level ground. The fact that it was raining hard meant that I could not be bothered to get my map out and check. By the time I finally admitted to myself that the route could not be right, the day was blown and I felt a right idiot.

The wind can be used in the same way as the slope. If you start a walk with the wind on your right cheek but half an hour later it is on your left cheek, stop for a minute and ask yourself why. Has the wind changed direction or are you walking in circles in the mist?

The most important aid to common sense, after slope, is timing: always have an idea of how long a leg of your walk should take, even on simple terrain and in good weather. In bad weather this becomes critical and should be carefully worked out by the formula already mentioned on page 93. Likewise an automatic ticking off of your check features will stop you going wrong. Remember that you cannot get lost if you know where you are!

# 7

# Walking techniques

This chapter covers many of the things that experienced back-packers and mountaineers do by instinct but those with less experience have to learn to do the hard way. It is hoped that this chapter will help you across that hurdle a little bit quicker.

## Fitness

When I was a youngster at the start of my walking career my father told me that I would get used to walking on the level within a day or two and to walking uphill after a couple of weeks, but that I would never get used to walking downhill. To this day he has always been proved right; if anything, as my joints have taken a pounding over the years the downhill bit has got harder and harder. On a long walking holiday such as trekking in Nepal or India, there is nothing wrong with setting easy days to start with and working gently up to full fitness. Obviously if your walking consists of nothing but the occasional weekend in the hills or out on the moors, then you don't have that option.

The best training for walking is to walk and that is something we can all do every day. In fact, after the jogging craze of a few years ago it is now thought that a lunchtime walk is as good an exercise as you can get. My mother walks every lunchtime and swears by it. Make walking an attitude of life; walk instead of taking the car half a mile to the newsagent, and walk upstairs instead of taking lifts and escalators: it is wonderful exercise.

However, I would advise against overdoing it. There is no need to pound out the miles on hard road surfaces whilst carrying heavy rucksacks and it can do irreparable harm to your knees and ankles over time.

## Feet

Getting your feet used to wearing boots will repay the effort. Although not as important now as when boots were big, heavy leather monsters, your feet will still need to get used to boots. Many people will give you home-spun ideas for hardening feet, such as soaking them in various concoctions. I have never tried any of these but, if they work for you, then why not?

### *Sore spots*

It is important to treat any sore spots as soon as they start. Sore spots (as opposed to blisters) are best treated by padding them with plasters, gauze pads and tape or specialist plaster such as 'Compeed'. Until the foot hardens up, protect the area by covering it with something like zinc oxide tape whenever you walk. Some people react to this type of tape and non-allergenic varieties are available although they do not seem to be as good. The treatment of blisters is considered in Chapter 9.

## Paths and trails

When you first start walking, stick to trails and footpaths until you are used to your rucksack, your boots and other gear – and your muscles are used to carrying it all. There are, however, major downsides with walking any path network. Firstly, they can be very muddy and when you are carrying great dollops of mud on your feet you will understand the old adage that every pound on your foot is worth ten on your back. I would never advocate straying off the path, especially if there is an access problem, but there are times when paths become impassable and you have to find an alternative. Many paths, usually through overuse, have reached such a state that they have been covered with raised wooden walkways which, although they make the walking easier, are hardly aesthetic.

The second problem, which is linked to the first, is that of erosion. A path becomes worn and loose, so people walk on the edges which in turn also become worn and loose. The problem goes on and on until the 'path' can be 10m (33ft) wide or more. Resist walking at the edges of paths and avoid cutting the corners where paths zigzag up hills.

## Walking uphill

The important story to remember about walking uphill is the parable of the hare and the tortoise: slow wins. The real trick when walking in the hills is to keep a steady pace, but change the length of your stride and do not stop. This may take some getting used to, the pace might seem to a fit youngster almost funereal and boring but it is a pace which can be kept up all day. Rushing on and stopping to rest all the time might seem faster but it is very draining and in the end will be much slower. It takes far more energy to stop, sit down and get up again than it does just to keep plodding. A good adage is that if you cannot talk to each other then you are going too fast.

Think about what you are doing with your hands and feet. Swinging your arms about is a waste of energy; try hitching your thumbs on your waist strap or putting your hands in your pockets (but not too deep — you might need to get them out in a hurry). Always try to place your feet flat when you are walking uphill. Many people are tempted to walk on their toes, which only uses the small calf muscles rather than the large thigh muscles that will be used by placing your whole foot down. Keeping your paces short will also use your leg muscles more efficiently.

The choice of whether to walk straight up a hill or zigzag up is one that comes with experience of your own abilities. In general, the steeper the hill the more need to zigzag up.

## Walking downhill

The worst thing about walking downhill is that it so often happens at the end of the day, when you are already tired and your legs are just starting to reach that jelly stage. Many people advocate running down on the double theory that it gets it over with quickly and that the pounding will be less if you are not trying to stop with each step. Although I might agree in the case of experts, this is a recipe for disaster for anyone else and the potential of flying head over heels with a large rucksack is all too real.

Try to avoid walking down very steep hills if you can. If there

7.1 Walkind down steep slopes: the correct position. Try to keep your body weight directly above your feet and resist the temptation to lean backwards.

is there a better route which is not so steep, take it, or zigzag down the hill. If you are committed to walking down a steep slope, then take it carefully as this is where most accidents happen in the hills. Avoid leaning backwards; it may feel like you are about to fall over but you will not. People fall when going downhill by leaning into the slope and falling on to their backs, but by leaning out you are simply keeping upright. Bend your knees to absorb the shock and dig your heels in. This is where square-cut heels come into their own.

It is important that you can see your feet when walking down slopes. Avoid high bracken where you will not know if your feet are about to get stuck behind a rock or, even worse, drop into a hole in the peat.

## Scree slopes

Scree, or talus, slopes are slopes of loose rocks varying from rucksack size or larger to small pebbles. They can vary from a short patch of a few metres to long runs down whole hillsides and are usually formed by the freeze/thaw actions in cracks in the rocks as a natural consequence of winter. Whatever their size or makeup, they should always be treated with respect. There are two dangers: falling over yourself, and sending stones down on top of someone else.

When a group is walking on scree, whether across, up or down, try to avoid having people above each other. Try walking in wide zigzags and let people catch up at the end of each leg. It is best if the whole party stays close together so that any dislodged stone can be stopped before it starts moving too fast. If someone should dislodge a stone, they should shout 'below' as loudly as possible to warn others below them.

There is a great temptation to run down scree slopes but this should be avoided. If a runner should catch a foot and fall over forwards, the damage would be horrendous, and falling backwards would probably result in a badly cut hand. Having said that, people will always run down scree; so, if you feel that you must, lean out so that you do not fall backwards, watch your feet and 'go with the flow'. A good scree runner will look almost like a downhill skier.

It should never be forgotten that scree slopes are in themselves valuable botanical sites where many plants species, some of them rare, make their homes. For this reason, if no other, they should be avoided if possible.

## Grass and bracken slopes

Wet grass and bracken are dangerously slippery and it can be almost impossible to stop yourself sliding if you fall over. When walking downhill, use the walking posture shown in figure 7.1 but exaggerate it even more so and dig your heels well in. Avoid the great temptation to sit and slide down slopes like this. Waterproofs and wet grass together give about as much friction as a pane of glass on an ice rink: unless you are absolutely sure that there is a gentle run out to the slope below, you could be in for a nasty surprise.

## Trekking poles

Trekking poles are the modern equivalent of walking-sticks. They are based on equipment used in ski-mountaineering and look like telescopic ski poles.

There are several advantages to using trekking poles (if used correctly): they can take up to 40 per cent of the shock away from your knees when walking downhill; they can be a huge aid when walking up slopes, giving you something to push on whilst staying upright; and they are wonderful at helping your balance in many situations. Poles will also help your breathing, as the act of holding them out and using them will open out your chest and help to work your lungs. Finally, they are wonderful for crossing streams – and you can lean on them when you stop walking!

The disadvantages are that, until you get used to them, there is a tendency to trip over them, which could be dangerous. Despite the temptation, they should not be used on steep snow slopes as it is impossible to apply them to stop a slide; get your ice axe out instead. The same applies on steep, rocky ground where the danger of them getting caught in a rock could be fatal. Put them away and use your hands instead. Avoid using poles on peaty bogs as there is a tendency for them to sink in and dump you on your face unless they are equipped with 'baskets' (plastic attachments near the tips which stop them penetrating wet ground or snow).

When choosing your poles, do not skimp on the money. Although they are expensive, they will be taking a lot of pounding and cheap poles will not be up to it. Look for a simple and

7.2 Using and holding trekking poles. Note that in this case the poles have been shortened because the walker is going uphill. For downhill walking the poles would be lengthened in order to keep the walker's elbow at right angles with the tip of the pole on the ground. Note also how the uphill foot is flat on the ground, thereby making use of the powerful thigh muscles rather than the weaker calf muscles.

effective telescopic action – they must be easily adjustable and should fold up small enough to fit into your rucksack. They need to be comfortable; the wrist straps should be easy to adjust and without any buckles digging into your hands. You will need baskets for wet ground but not for rocky ground, so find poles with baskets that can be easily removed. Some poles now have a sprung tip that is supposed to take the shock out of using them, which makes sense although I have not tried them. Given the cost of poles, it might well be worth borrowing a pair for a few days as they are not for everyone.

Poles should be used as a pair (not singly like a walking-stick) and should be held properly in a ski grip as shown in figure 7.2. The length needs to be adjusted so that when the tip is on the ground your arm is bent at a right angle at the elbow. This is where the adjustment comes in as they will need to be shortened when going uphill and they will need to be longer when going downhill. In use they should be placed in a positive manner and not just waved about. Think about each placement, which should be just in front of you and on ground as firm as possible. Use them smoothly with opposing arms and legs in a definite manner. Concentrate on transferring weight on to each pole as it is placed. It does take some getting used to but I believe that the results are well worth it.

## Walking in the snow

Walking in winter conditions of snow and ice is really only for the experienced and, possibly, trained mountaineer. The skills involved cannot really be learnt from a book and in any case are outside the scope of this one. (The *Outward Bound Walker's Handbook* covers winter walking in more detail.) However, many winter walks do not go above the snow line for more than short periods and so it would be wrong to exclude them here.

The first rule is that all snow conditions demand great respect. Get a weather and avalanche forecast each and every time before you go on the hills and pay attention to them. Listen to local knowledge about which areas are safe and find out what the weather has been doing recently; recent heavy snowfall or warm weather are two indicators that the snow pack may be unsafe. If you are not sure, then go somewhere else: the mountains will still be there next year.

Although simple walking does not usually require crampons unless the ground is steep, you must have an ice axe if you are going on snow and you must know how to use it.

Walking up and down hard snow slopes is a little like walking on grass slopes. Use a good kicking action to get a good purchase and keep upright. Groups should walk in single file, treading in each other's footsteps. The leader should be changed at regular intervals – it is hard work being in front in snow! Have your ice axe out and carried in the uphill hand ready for use. If you are zigzagging up a slope there is a moment at the end of each leg where the axe will have to be changed from one hand to the other. This can be tricky and takes some practice. Whether or not to use wrist straps is a personal choice but they do ensure that the axe will not be torn out of your grip if you fall.

## Kicking steps

As the slopes get steeper or harder, you will need to start kicking steps (figure 7.3). There is an art to this but it is easily learnt. You need heavy, stiff boots (plastic boots are best but you are unlikely to be wearing these unless you are into winter mountaineering). Move up the slope in short zigzags, facing side on to the slope and using the side of the boot in a sawing motion at right angles to the slope. The steps should be close together and you need to cross and uncross your feet at each step so the outside edge of the top boot kicks the top step, the lower foot is then crossed in front of that foot and the inside edge of what was the lower boot is used to kick the next step. If you feel insecure, you can progress sideways with the lower foot moving into the step left by the top foot (this means that you will take twice as many steps).

Ice axe planted in snow

Outside edge kicking step

7.3  Kicking steps.

If you are kicking steps downhill they will need to be even closer together, as it is harder to balance moving down to each step. Crossing your feet is not usually a good option when going down. The easiest method if the slope is not too steep, is to keep your legs fairly rigid, driving your heels well in with each step and keeping your body well upright.

If the snow surface is too hard to kick steps, use your ice axe to cut them. The technique is simple but worth practising. With the axe in your uphill hand, use a good swing so that the head of the axe just glances the surface of the snow, rather than digging into it. A good horizontally cut step need not be more than 3–5cm (1–2in) deep to be more than adequate. When cutting steps, make progress on the hill in the same way as if you were kicking steps.

## Using the ice axe

Perhaps the most important skill in winter walking is to be able to use an ice axe effectively. There are two sides to this: using it for support, and stopping a slide if you should fall over.

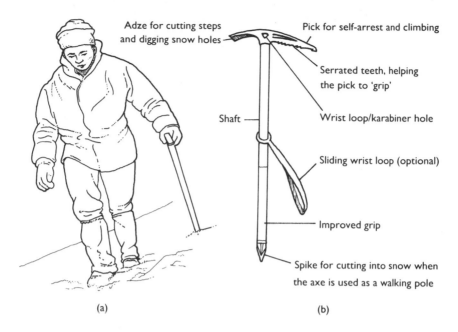

Adze for cutting steps and digging snow holes

Pick for self-arrest and climbing

Serrated teeth, helping the pick to 'grip'

Shaft

Wrist loop/karabiner hole

Sliding wrist loop (optional)

Improved grip

Spike for cutting into snow when the axe is used as a walking pole

(a)                                                    (b)

**7.4** (a) Using an ice axe for support. (b) Parts of an ice axe. Note that sliding wrist loops are less common now; the sling or loop is usually tied directly into the wrist loop/ karabiner hole.

When walking, always carry the axe in your uphill hand with the hand over the top of the pick, which should be facing backwards. In this position the axe is always ready for use as a brake if you should fall over. To choose the correct length of an axe, hold it in this position; the spike on the bottom should just brush the ground on a gentle slope. About 55–65cm (21–25in) seems to be right for most people; shorter axes are used for climbing rather than walking. As with trekking poles, use the axe in a positive manner and put some thought into each placement rather than just letting it drag on the slope beside you.

## Stopping a slide

The ice axe will come into its own if you should fall over and start to slide. It is the only piece of equipment you have that will stop you hurtling down a steep slope. The first aim when sliding is to get into the self-arrest position shown in figure 7.5.

The feet need to be lifted well clear of the ground at all times to prevent them catching the snow and sending you cartwheeling. Arch your back, as this will dig your knees into the slope and help to force the axe in. The axe should be across your body with the adze pressed against your shoulder (you will know if you are doing this right because the adze will leave its mark on you!). The pick of the axe should be pushed slowly into the slope. Do not jerk it in or the axe will be torn out of your hands.

If you are lucky you will fall into this face-down, feet-down position. If not, you must get yourself into it.

**7.5** The correct position for self-arresting a slide.

## To get into position:

- If you are on your back, roll over towards the *top* of the axe so that the bottom spike does not dig in.

- If you are falling face first, place the axe out to one side at shoulder height and dig the pick in. This will spin you around into a position where you can remove the axe and start the normal self-arrest procedure.

- If the worst happens and you are head down and on your back, you should get on to your front first and then spin around.

- If you are rolling rather than sliding, spread your arms and legs into a wide cartwheel position. This will stop the roll and allow you to self-arrest.

No matter how experienced, everybody should practise self-arresting with an ice axe at the start of each winter. It is a life-saving technique which needs to be done instinctively and well if it is to work.

# 8

## Hazards and emergencies

It is quite possible that you can spend your entire walking career without ever coming across a dangerous or emergency situation, but it is unlikely. Your first step away from the waymarked paths and tracks takes you into an environment where you need to be able to recognize hazards and a wide variety of potential dangers. In different parts of the world I have had to contend with a student with heat stroke; I have been so badly bitten by sandflies and mosquitos that I was unable to work; I have been mauled by a water buffalo; and at home in Britain I have been involved in the rescue of a number of hill walkers with a variety of injuries.

## Weather

The weather can at times become a real menace. I was once caught in a violent lightning storm in the Picos mountains of Northern Spain which felt like being under heavy gun fire. There are two types of weather hazard: those caused directly by the weather, such as lightning, and those caused in a more indirect manner such as a river in spate.

### Lightning

Lightning strikes are very rare but they do happen. Apart from the obvious signs of a storm, if you are about to get caught in a major electrical storm you will notice that the air becomes charged and you will feel it in your hair and on metal objects. The first and most important rule is to get away from any exposed position that you may be in, be that on a mountain top or standing under a tall tree. Some people will tell you to discard metal objects such as ice axes but this would be foolish as you might need them after the storm has passed. Instead, place obvious metal objects away from you and if possible untie yourself from wet ropes which are good lightning conductors.

The best place to sit out a storm, although it may be unpleasant, is on the open ground. Sit on your rucksack and tuck your knees up to your chin to reduce your target size and provide a short path for lightning should you get struck. Avoid sitting in cave entrances or under boulders where you might act as the electricity conductor in a spark gap.

## Storms

A storm does not have to be electrical to present a hazard, nor does it have to be violent. Strong winds by themselves can be not only a major impediment to walking but also a hazard in their own right. Avoid ridges and wind gaps if at all possible. If you get caught on the hilltops keep in the lee of the ridges and drop down as soon as possible. The exception is if there is a lot of snow on the ground when lee (i.e. downwind,) slopes may present a cornice danger (see page 118) and should be avoided.

You should also be aware that the wind will reduce the air temperature in a dramatic fashion. A mild day of +5°C (41°F) will be reduced by windchill to an equivalent of −2°C (28°F) in winds as light as 10kph (6mph).

Perhaps the biggest danger in heavy rain is that everyone in the group pulls their hoods up tight and retreats into their own worlds. Navigation and watching out for each other become even more important at this stage.

## White-outs

Many people refer to low visibility as being in a white-out, which is not the case. A true white-out is where the ground and air become indistinguishable from each other, such as in wind-blown snow. The best answer to a true white-out is to put up your tent and sit it out. The second, and riskier, solution is to navigate through it. In this case have a single person on the rope well out in front of the group, with the rope taut and tied to the rest of the group. If you do decide to navigate through a white-out it will the best test of your micro-nav skills you will ever experience and should not be underestimated.

## Floods and rivers

One of the biggest dangers that the weather brings is that of flooding. As well as affecting your choice of camp-site (see page 52), it makes the crossing of rivers a major problem.

The first rule to be observed when crossing rivers in spate is: don't. If at all possible, avoid crossing any river which is fast-moving and higher than your knees. Trying to cross a fast-moving river which is higher than your waist is approaching the suicidal. If you have decided that a river must be crossed, there are a number of procedures which can help.

First keep your boots on, although you could remove your socks. Take off any baggy waterproofs which are going to catch the water. If possible, pass rucksacks across, but if they have to be carried you should loosen the shoulder straps and undo the waist and chest straps so the sack can be dropped if necessary.

Although there are many ways of crossing without a rope, they are all better suited to slower-moving water because they require a number of people to move together, which, is extremely diffi-cult in a fast-moving river. Look for a suitable spot at which to cross; it should have low banks, no obstacles such as boulders or trees and it should not be on the bend of a river, where the cur-rent runs faster.

There are several methods of using the rope, each of which has its own merits. Figure 8.1 shows my personal favourite, in which the aim is to keep the rope in a triangular shape over the water.

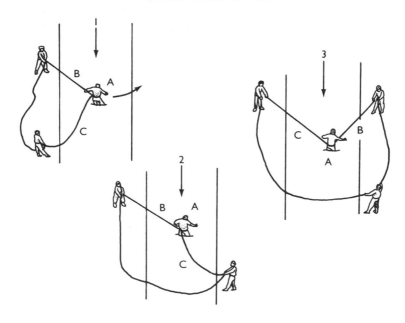

**8.1** Crossing a river. The person crossing (A), leans back on the top rope (B) for support. This rope is fixed and swings across like a pendulum. The lower rope (C) is paid out and is used to pull the crosser back to shore should they fall in. The first person, once across, can take over the role of controlling the lower rope, whilst the second person across can take over the control of the top rope. If there are more than three in a group, it is important that someone keeps hold of the rope on the first bank in order to pull it back each time.

However, you should only use a rope to cross a river in spate as a last resort. If you must, remember to give support from upstream, pull out anyone who has fallen in from downstream, and *never* let the rope jam. If it does, be prepared to cut it.

## Loose rock

Loose rock is found in a number of places. The biggest area is found on scree, or talus, slopes; this is covered on page 105.

Other dangers associated with loose rock are walking under it and tripping over it. It is only common sense to avoid camping or taking a break under a crag with loose rock on it. However, the hazard is not always easy to spot and care does need to be taken in mountain

regions. Loose rock underfoot is usually safe to walk on with care –
if you can see it. When hidden by high bracken it is hard work,
time-consuming and a potential area for sprained ankles.

## Snow, ice, cornices and crevasses

Ice, cornices and crevasses are hazards that you should not
encounter in the passage of a normal backpacking trip. Some
trails do, however, cross the lower levels of glaciers, where you
should always stick to the marked trails and seek local advice. On
ridges and mountain plateaux, avoid lee slopes if there is snow
on the ground. The temptation to slide down snow and ice
slopes, fun though it is, should also be avoided; at least until you
have totally mastered the art of ice axe control. There is a short
section on crossing snow fields on page 108.

## Wildlife

Wildlife is usually more of a nuisance than a hazard and most
wild animals will leave you alone if you leave them alone. Be
aware of the habitat and habits of any local nasties. For example: avoid holes under stones and boulders if you are in snake
country, and find out from local people in advance the best way
to act in bear country, including what precautions need to be
taken when cooking. A good tip is to copy the locals: whilst
working at Outward Bound Hong Kong I wondered why all the
staff carried large sticks, and I soon discovered that the sticks
not only kept the packs of semi-wild dogs at bay but were also
swung in front of your face to avoid a surprise encounter with
woodland spiders.

If confronted with dogs, the answer seems to be to stay calm
and back away. Shouting just gets animals excited, although
throwing stones will often disperse a pack of agitated dogs. If the
worst happens and you get bitten whilst in a rabies area, you
must get to medical help with all speed. Rabies immunization

does not actually prevent the disease; it merely slows it down to give you more time to get help.

Mosquito and midge bites are covered on page 139.

## Disease, foul water and food

In many parts of the world, disease is spread in alarming ways by food and water.

### *Water*

Always regard water with a degree of suspicion until you know for certain that it is safe to drink. Just because locals drink it does not mean that you can. At best it takes time to get used to different water supplies; at worst they can carry all manner of unpleasant surprises. If you are unsure of it, water should always be well boiled for several minutes. If you want cold water, boil it at night and leave it to cool – but do not leave it cooling in plastic bottles as it will taste awful. Water-purifying tablets have a limited benefit but will often be enough, although they do make the water taste like a swimming pool. Adding iodine is another method which works but leaves the water tasting awful. There are some good filters on the market which are very effective though the cheap ones will not be up to the job.

### *Food*

Unless you are sure of your food, follow the simple maxim: 'Peel it, cook it or leave it.' Whilst this might apply to food stalls in, say, India and Thailand there is rarely any need to worry about food on backpacking trips. Avoid leaving food to cool and then reheating it as this could lead to infection. Unless you are an expert, do not experiment with food harvested along the trail. In particular be careful with seafood such as cockles and mussels: sea creatures contain some of the strongest poisons known.

## Accidents

As well as the hazards already outlined, there are many accidents resulting from lack of concentration, lack of technique and experience, or sheer bad luck. Chapter 9, on first aid, explains what immediate steps to take crisis where life is at risk; it also deals with bleeding, burns, shock, hypothermia and heat exhaustion, sprains and fractures, frostbite, stings, blisters and certain medical conditions. Whatever the problem, you need to remain calm in order to be competent, and it helps if you have a logical emergency procedure well rehearsed in your mind before you set out.

## Emergency procedure

If the worst should happen and you are involved in a medical emergency, such as hypothermia or a broken leg, the first rule to remember is, 'Don't panic'. This may not be easy but in any situation it is vital that you act rationally and calmly. Force yourself to take a few deep breaths and 'relax' before you start making decisions on which lives might depend. The best way of staying calm is by knowing the emergency procedure well enough that you can switch into auto pilot.

---

**The stages of emergency procedure are:**

---

1. Stop.

2. Assess.

3. Remove to safety

4. Provide immediate life-saving first aid.

5. Provide shelter, and assume hypothermia and shock.

6. Provide warmth.

7. Send for help.

---

There is rarely, if ever, any point in pressing on and hoping that things will cure themselves as if by magic.

Assessing the situation may sound simple but a few seconds spent working out what is actually wrong can save hours later. First, check for the *safety* of the casualty, yourself and the rest of the party. For example: is there any danger of falling stones? Are you on a loose scree slope? Might somebody fall off the edge of a cliff? Is the group or casualty too close to a river? Then check the *condition* of the casualty, yourself and the rest of the party. Use the body check method on page 126 of the First Aid section.

It may be essential to move to safer ground (e.g. if you are on steep, loose scree). The technique used for moving/turning a casualty with neck or back injuries is outlined on pages 123–4. Other emergency procedures are outlined in Chapter 9.

In addition, before going out you must know who coordinates the rescue services in your area so that the group going for help can dial the appropriate emergency number. In the UK, for example, you should dial 999 and ask for the police, who call out and coordinate rescues, although the teams are actually unpaid amateurs. In the USA, the ranger service often both controls and forms the rescue team and in Europe, professional mountain guides carry out rescues. While rescues in the UK are free, other countries (including Europe and the USA) charge for the rescue services. (Check that your insurance gives you ample cover to pay for a call-out, before you need to do so.)

Those who remain at the site of the incident must be prepared for a long wait. It may be several hours before a rescue team arrives. Ensure that you sustain morale by keeping the kettle on the boil and having people talk to each other. Also keep monitoring the condition of the casualty and of your group.

Finally, it is a common mistake to call for help from your home base in order to keep incidents out of the press, or even avoiding a call-out completely and hoping that 'things will get better'. You must ask which is the greater embarrassment: a premature call-out, or a dead casualty who might have been saved?

# 9

# First aid

No responsible person should head for the great outdoors until they have been on a recognized first aid training course. The Red Cross, the St John Ambulance and the St Andrew's Ambulance Association all run excellent courses and the telephone number of your nearest local branch can be found in the telephone directory. Many of the key techniques used in first aid – especially mouth-to-mouth ventilation and chest compression cannot be learned from books and must be practised under the supervision of a qualified trainer. Books, including this one and the more detailed *Outward Bound First Aid Handbook*, should be regarded as reference works rather than as substitutes for training.

Often the best emergency first aid action is to do nothing at all, other than minimize the danger to the patient and seek qualified help at once. You can do a great deal of harm by over-enthusiastic medical treatment. For this reason, this section deals with lifesaving procedures and the treatment of minor ailments but it does not go into in-depth diagnosis, or procedures such as tensioning broken limbs.

---

**The emphasis in your first aid should be to:**

---

- Preserve the life of the victim.

- Prevent any further harm or deterioration.

- Send promptly for qualified help.

- Promote recovery, if within your means.

---

The proper order in which you should carry out first aid procedures is:

1. Safety.

2. Body check.

3. Cardiopulmonary resuscitation (CPR).

4. Bleeding

5. Burns.

6. Shock and hypothermia.

7. Other injuries and conditions.

## Safety

Your first thought when approaching any victim is to make the accident area safe for yourself and other people. For example: if the casualty has had an electrical shock and is still touching a live lead, it will help nobody if you get electrocuted yourself. Check all around and above the victim for any signs of danger. Switch off the electrical current, activate fire alarms or open windows to release any smoke or fumes. Only once all risks have been eliminated, approach the casualty.

Never move a patient with a spinal injury, except as a last resort. If it is essential that the victim be moved at once (because of the danger of falling rocks, for example) great care must be taken, especially if it looks as though the victim has a damaged neck or spine. Quick indicators of a possible spinal injury are the nature of the accident, the position in which the victim is lying, and the lack of any sensation in the limbs.

___

**When turning or lifting a victim with a suspected spinal injury:**
___

• Use at least three or four people acting together.

Plenty of support at the spine

Never release support at the head

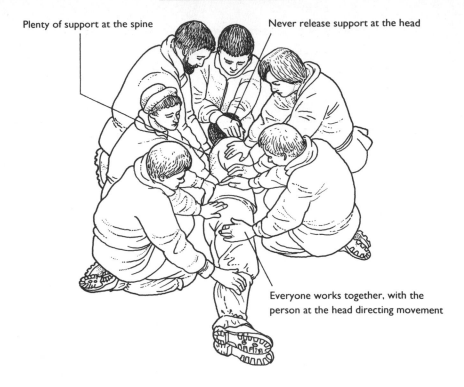

Everyone works together, with the
person at the head directing movement

**9.1** The correct way to turn or lift a victim with a spinal injury.

- Move head, trunk and legs together, keeping the head supported.

- Avoid any rotation or bending of the spine.

A victim who needs to be moved can be rolled (as shown in figure 9.1) onto a stretcher or board (if available). Moving a spinal victim is best left to experts, and unless there is a very immediate risk to life and limb, it is better not to attempt this at all.

## Assessing the casualty

The next step is to perform a body check to ascertain the actual damage. To a large extent this is the most important element of first aid. The very first question you need to ask is whether the patient is conscious or not. If more than one patient is injured, always attend to the unconscious ones first; your priority being to see that they can breathe.

---

**Remember your priorities by the maxim Airway, Breathing, Circulation (ABC):**

---

- Airway
  If the casualty is unconscious, check that the airway is clear. Noisy breathing is an indication that the airway is blocked. Remove from the mouth any obstruction, such as loose dentures or mud. Tilt the head back by gently lifting the chin; this will clear the tongue from the back of the throat and open the airway.
- Breathing
  Place your ear near the victim's mouth. Can you hear breathing or feel any breath on your cheek? While doing this place your hand gently on the abdomen and look along the body. Can you feel the abdomen rising and falling or see the chest doing the same?
- Circulation
  At the same time feel for the victim's pulse by placing your fingertips (not thumb) on the neck, just behind the Adam's apple, in the gap between the windpipe and the muscle alongside it.

---

If the three ABC checks show a problem with the breathing or circulation then you need to take immediate action. If you cannot detect a pulse, waste no time in seeking help. Get to the nearest telephone and call an ambulance, leaving the patient alone if necessary (this is the *only* occasion on which you should consider leaving the patient alone). On returning to the patient, give mouth-to-mouth ventilation and chest compression until help arrives (these lifesaving techniques are designed to maintain the oxygen supply to the brain until the medical team arrives). To learn how to use these resuscitation techniques you should attend a first aid course.

## The body check

If the victim is fully conscious, and there are no problems with the ABC checks, continue with the body check. This is simply a case of working down the body and looking for signs of injuries. While doing so you should talk to the casualty (do this even if they are unconscious; they may be much more aware than you think). Reassure them, explain what you are doing and ask them to tell you if anything you do hurts them. Watch their face to see if the expression changes as you touch parts of the body. Ask for the history of the accident if you did not see it, and ask whether anyone else was involved (there may be another victim lying unconscious nearby). Always remember that the obvious injury may not be the life-threatening one.

### Head

Always start at the head. Look for any obvious injury and check for blood or fluid coming from the ears or nose which might indicate damage inside the skull. Check the eyes for foreign bodies or damage and the pupils for comparative size and reaction to light (which might indicate concussion). Feel if the skin is hot, cold, clammy or dry. These, together with other signs, could suggest hypothermia, heatstroke and/or shock. Finally be aware of the breathing: is it fast or slow, deep or shallow, and is it regular or struggling?

### Neck

Move down to the neck and feel around for any obvious injury or dampness from bleeding. Check to see if the casualty is wearing a warning medallion such as those worn by diabetics or epileptics. Be aware of the pulse rate.

## Trunk

Working on both sides of the trunk, press the ribs in carefully to see if there is a reaction by the victim which would indicate a chest or rib injury. Feel for abnormal hardness in the abdomen. Feel under the back for obvious injury, deformity or dampness from bleeding.

## Limbs

Work along the arms and then the legs feeling for any unusual limb position, swelling, or bleeding. Check for a warning bracelet indicating diabetes, epilepsy, etc. See if the casualty can move the arms, legs, fingers and toes. If not, ask where the pain or difficulty lie.

## Diagnosis

This body check only takes a few minutes, but it could be a life-saver. Having made the check you are in a better position to inform the rescue services of the likely nature of the problem, so that they can gauge the level of their response.

# The recovery position

Once the initial checks have been completed, the victim needs to be placed in the recovery position – unless suffering from a spinal injury (see pages 123–4) – to prevent them choking on their own vomit or ingesting the acids produced by the stomach.

Kneeling beside the casualty, straighten the legs. Place the arm nearest to you at right angles to the casualty's body, then bend the upper arm parallel with the body, with the palm facing up. All the time ensure that the head is kept tilted back and the airway clear. Bring the arm furthest away from you across the casualty's chest and place their hand against the cheek nearest to

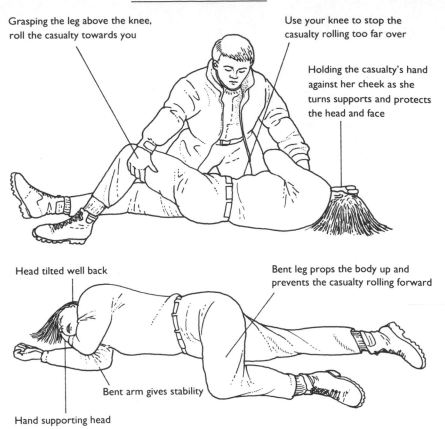

Grasping the leg above the knee, roll the casualty towards you

Use your knee to stop the casualty rolling too far over

Holding the casualty's hand against her cheek as she turns supports and protects the head and face

Head tilted well back

Bent leg props the body up and prevents the casualty rolling forward

Bent arm gives stability

Hand supporting head

**9.2** The recovery position.

you, with the palm facing outwards. This will cushion the patient's face and head when they are rolled over. Using your other hand, hold the thigh furthest from you and, keeping the casualty's foot flat on the floor, draw up the knee. Keeping the casualty's hand pressed against their cheek, pull the raised thigh towards you. This will roll the casualty neatly into the correct recovery position.

Ensure that the head is kept tilted back and supported on the casualty's hand. Once in this position the casualty should never be left alone but should be closely monitored for breathing problems or the state of their consciousness.

# Getting help

Prompt action on the part of trained medics is the key to preventing the loss of life in emergencies. This is vital so it is well worth taking a mobile telephone with you on any expedition to call out the rescue services if anything goes wrong. Be sure that the batteries are fully charged and that the telephone is protected from wet and damage by wrapping it in padding and plastic bags. Be sure that members of your party know where the telephone is, how to use it, and what numbers to call to summon help.

If you are unable to take this precaution, you should ideally choose two competent members of your party to summon help, while the remainder stay with the casualty. Make sure that they go fully equipped as a self-contained party with map, compass shelter, etc. Of course, if there are only two of you, the decision whether to stay with or leave the patient is extremely difficult, and will depend on factors such as the weather, how far you are from habitation and the nature of the patient's injuries. If you stay with the patient, you can use a whistle or torch to attract attention. (Six long blasts or flashes are the internationally recognized distress calls; these are answered with three short blasts or flashes).

Make sure that those who go to summon help know the patient's precise location. If you are unsure of the exact grid reference, you can at least make a note of prominent landmarks in the area and take compass bearings from them to find your approximate position.

---

**Be prepared to give the following information to the rescue services:**

- Numbers and names of casualties, and the name of your organization.

- Precise location, including description.

- Your assessment of the nature of their injuries.

- The age, condition and state of mind of the casualties.

- Time of accident and weather conditions at the scene.

- Details of the equipment available at the site.

---

## Specific procedures

Once you have sent for help you can begin to treat the patient's injuries.

### Bleeding

Blood loss should be attended to rapidly. Internal bleeding is revealed by a number of signs, which may include bruising, discolouring and/or bleeding from the body openings. There is little you can do to treat internal bleeding except for treating the shock that will almost certainly accompany it (see page 132).

The treating of external bleeding is more straightforward. Remember two things: elevation and direct pressure. Elevating the wound will help to slow the rate of blood flow. Direct pressure can be applied to the wound with anything available. In the case of major bleeding, hygiene comes a low second so do not be afraid to use your hand tight against the wound or use a dirty rag, if that is all that is available; any risk of infection can be worried about later.

Get a dressing on the wound straightaway, but do not bind the wound too tightly; your aim is to stop the bleeding, not cut off the blood supply to the limbs. If blood starts to seep through the first dressing, place another dressing directly on top of it. Do not remove the first dressing.

### Burns

Burns resulting from the misuse of stoves are common enough among backpackers. There is only one first aid treatment for burns, no matter what the severity: the whole wound should be immersed in cold, preferably running, water. Remove anything that is in the way of the burn (clothing, rings, watches and so on) but never try to remove anything that is actually sticking to the burn, such as clothing. The wound area should be left in the water for at least 10 minutes, and considerably longer for anything more than a very minor burn. Do not stop treatment just because the wound stops hurting; keep it in the water for a good few minutes after that. Prompt treatment of even a serious burn will have dramatic beneficial effects.

Never apply lotions, ointments or creams to any burn. One of the worst misapprehensions in first aid is that fat (such as butter or margarine) cools a burn. This may be the initial effect but the longer term effect is that the wound literally cooks in the fat.

If the skin on the burn in not broken, it should be left open to the air. If the skin is blistered or broken, use a clean, light dressing made of non-fluffy material to cover the wound and keep out infection. Plastic kitchen film makes an ideal burns dressing, or you could use a clean plastic bag.

Scalds, caused by hot liquids, should be treated in the same way. Treat any burns victims for shock (see page 132) and keep a close check that the airway does not become obstructed while the patient is lying down to recover.

## Sunburn

Prevention is far better than cure for this condition, so wear protective clothing and use sun blocks on exposed and vulnerable areas, such as the back of the neck, the face and lips, and the feet. After-sun lotions and calamine lotion will help to relieve minor burning.

## Shock and hypothermia

These conditions can be killers in their own right. They can also be the underlying (and more serious) problem in an accident. In both instances, the first safeguard is protection from the elements. Shelter can take a variety of forms, but tents are the obvious choice if you are carrying them. If not, a group emergency shelter is a good second choice.

As a last resort, survival bags are infinitely better than nothing. A survival bag is a large, heavyweight plastic bag. To use it as an emergency shelter (figure 9.3), cut out a small hole for your face and pull it over your head. Tuck it in neatly around you and sit on it, using your sleeping mat or sack liner to insulate you from the ground. Pull your rucksack up over your legs. If the bag is large enough for two people, the warmth factor increases considerably.

**Shock**

With anything more than a minor injury or accident, it is safe to assume that the patient will have suffered some degree of shock.

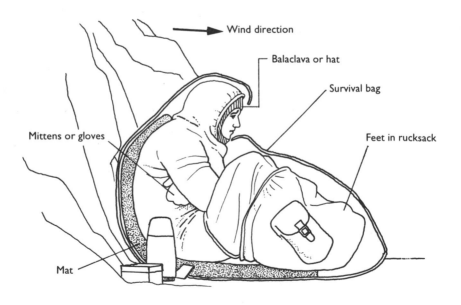

**9.3** Using a survival bag as an emergency shelter.

As well as the actual casualty, other members of the party should be closely monitored in case they, too, develop the symptoms of shock.

---

### The initial signs of shock are:

---

- A rapid pulse.

- Pale, grey skin. A fingernail or earlobe, if pressed, does not regain its colour immediately.

- Sweating and cold, clammy skin.

---

As the shock develops, patients will become weak, giddy and nauseous. They may vomit, and their breathing becomes rapid and shallow. The pulse continues to be fast but irregular.

If the patient is not treated, they will become restless, anxious or aggressive. They may suffer 'air hunger', yawning and gasping for air. In the most severe case they may become unconscious and eventually the heart will stop beating.

The treatment for shock is surprisingly simple and effective. First, treat the obvious cause of shock, such as bleeding or burns. Lie the casualty down, keeping the head low and raising the feet to aid the supply of blood to the brain. Loosen any tight clothing, belts or equipment. Keep the casualty warm and insulated, give them plenty of reassurance and send for help.

Do not let the casualty move about, eat, drink or smoke. If they complain of being thirsty, moisten their lips with water.

## Hypothermia
Hypothermia or exposure, as it is commonly known, is one of the great killers on the hills but it can usually be avoided. It is caused by a combination of wet and cold, which can be aggravated by factors such as tiredness, inadequate clothing, inadequate diet and physical and mental attitude. Prevention is largely a matter of common sense.

## Before going on the hill ensure that:

- All members of the group are correctly clothed and equipped.

- Everyone has had a decent breakfast and has an adequate supply of food and drink (including emergency rations).

- The weather conditions are suitable for your planned trip.

- The planned route is within the physical and mental capabilities of all members of the group.

- No group member has a severe cold, flu or any other condition which makes the planned trip unsuitable for them.

On the trip the members of the group should always keep an eye on each other. No matter how bad the conditions get, it is vital to keep talking to each other. Hypothermia often goes unnoticed until too late because everybody in the group walks along enveloped in their own private world.

## The signs of hypothermia include:

- Shivering and cold, pale marble-like skin.

- Apathy, confusion and irrational or 'drunken' behaviour.

- Complaining of tiredness, coldness, cramp (particularly in the calf muscles) or blurred vision.

Many of these symptoms could also be attributed to being merely 'cold, wet and tired'. The key to early recognition of hypothermia depends upon knowing the members of your group and detecting behaviour that is out of character. The later signs, such as loss of faculties and blurred vision, are more obvious but the patient's health will already have deteriorated by the time these symptoms are displayed, and so the aim is to arrest hypothermia at a much earlier stage.

## The treatment for hypothermia:

- Stop at once. There is no point in pushing on unless you are very close to your base.

- Provide shelter from the elements. The priority is to get the casualty out of the wind or rain.

- Provide insulation from above and below.

- Start gentle rewarming. Placing another person in a sleeping bag with the casualty is a good method.

- Send for help.

You should never give the patient alcohol; nor should you attempt to rewarm the casualty rapidly by rubbing the skin or applying hot water bottles or any other form of direct heat. Give the patient a hot drink, soup or small amounts of high-energy food, such as chocolate, as long as there are not abdominal injuries. If there are other injuries, be cautious about food and drink but remember that hypothermia is often a bigger problem than the injury that started the situation.

Wet clothes should only be removed in a warm sheltered environment and only if there are dry clothes immediately at hand. However, many modern fibres are still warm when wet, and stripping a casualty off in wet, cold conditions in order to put them into dry clothes could be counter-productive. Having said that, there is little that is as good for morale as warm, dry clothes. Always assume that you and the other members of the group are also suffering from the initial stages of hypothermia and treat everyone accordingly. Remember: shelter, warmth and high morale are what you need to maintain while you wait for help.

## Frostbite

Frostnip, and the more serious condition of frostbite, can be treated by gentle rewarming if spotted early. The first signs are tingling in the affected parts, which become pale and numb. Frostnip is quite common and not a problem if treated. Frostbite, however, goes deeper into the body tissue, which turns hard, white and stiff, then mottled blue and eventually black.

In both cases, get medical help as soon as possible. Do not attempt to thaw out the affected part until there is no risk of refreezing, but seek warm surroundings quickly. Gently remove gloves, boots, socks, rings or watches and warm the area with your hands, in your lap or in the patient's armpits. Warm water can be used, but take care when drying – do not use pressure or burst any blisters.

## Acute mountain sickness

Acute mountain sickness (AMS) is a very serious, but specialized, condition caused by the effects of high altitude. Always seek specialist advice before going to high altitude (usually 3000m/9842ft and above). However, the two main points are one, ascend slowly and avoid an increase in sleeping altitude of more than 1000m/3281ft. After such an increase, spend a few days acclimatizing. And two, headaches, nausea and breathlessness are early signs of AMS. If experienced, you should descend at least 1000m/3281ft to avoid a more serious condition.

## Heat exhaustion

Heat exhaustion results from dehydration and salt loss because of excessive sweating. It can be caused by other conditions, such as diarrhoea or vomiting. Patients suffering from heat exhaustion will complain of dizziness, headaches, cramps and loss of appetite or nausea. The skin will be clammy, sweaty and pale. Move the patient to cool, shaded surroundings, preferably with a breeze. Help the patient to lie down, then raise and support the legs to promote blood flow to the brain. Give the patient as much salt solution (2 teaspoons of salt per 1 litre/2 pints of cool water) as they can drink. If recovery is slow, or if the patient's breathing and pulse remain rapid, seek immediate medical advice.

## Sprained ankles

Along with blisters (see page 140), sprained ankles are perhaps the most common walking injury. Although some sprains are major and very painful, most can be walked on after simple treatment and care. As the main cause of sprained ankles is going over on to the side of your foot, it follows that a good pair of boots with ankle support is the best prevention. Prompt treatment is the key to treatment of any sprain injury.

---

**Treatment is summed up in the mnemonic RICE:**

---

- **R**est.

- **I**ce (cooling the injured area in any suitable way).

- **C**ompression (strapping the ankle).

- **E**levation (raising the foot).

---

To strap an ankle: use an elastic or crepe bandage, start inside the instep of the foot and wrap the bandage tightly (but not too tightly) over the foot and around the ankle, continuing in a figure-of-eight around the foot and ankle until the foot is well supported. If possible, replace the boot to give additional support. Paracetamol can help with pain relief.

## Fractures

Fractures can be classified as those you can treat and walk with and those you cannot.

In the case of a minor fracture (for example of the arm, fingers or collar bone) there is usually no need to call out a rescue party. The fracture should be supported in whatever position the casualty finds most comfortable and restrained from further movement. Fingers can be strapped to each other, while a broken arm can be supported in a sling and then strapped to the body. A collar bone is treated in the same manner as if the arm on that side were broken. Minor foot, leg or ankle injuries can be treated similarly if the group is capable of helping the casualty back off the hill.

If the fracture cannot be treated, you should make the patient as comfortable as possible and summon help. If it is necessary to immobilize a limb to prevent the condition becoming worse, the best option is to use other body parts – strapping the legs together, for example. To do this, you need to place cushioning material between the legs, especially at the knees and ankles, then bandage the legs together, tying the knots on the side of the uninjured leg. Check that the bandages are not too tight by pinching a toe nail: if it stays pale, loosen and retie the bandages.

Do not give food or drink to the patient, in case they need an emergency operation to reset the bones.

## Dislocations

Dislocations can be very painful and require expert help. The exception, as with fractures, is in minor cases where the affected limb can be supported and the patient can still walk. Some people have a history of dislocations and sometimes know how to treat themselves by pushing the joint back in. This is very rare and is not something you should attempt.

## Chronic conditions

You should always be aware if any member of your party suffers from a chronic condition such as asthma, diabetes or epilepsy. In each case it is vital that you know how to deal with any problems that might arise, and that you have taken adequate supplies of medicines and inhalers. Asthma sufferers should carry and use their own inhalers rather than a communal one.

## Bites and stings

Bites and stings vary greatly from the intense annoyance caused by the Scottish midge to the lethal effects of some snakes and marine life. Black flies, midges, no-see-'ems and sand flies all have an unpleasant bite which is best avoided by keeping well covered and staying inside your tent at dusk and dawn, when they are most active. Repellent creams are not very effective and can harm your skin. Antihistamine lotions and pills may help to reduce the itching from insect bites but should not be used to excess.

Stings from insects (such as wasps and bees) or sea creatures (such as jellyfish, weaver fish or anemones) are usually more painful than dangerous, but be alert to multiple stings which have dangerous cumulative effects, stings to the mouth or throat that can swell and block the airway, and stings to people who develop an allergic reaction.

For a sting to the mouth, give the patient ice to suck if at all possible to reduce the swelling and get them to hospital. Multiple stings and allergic reactions manifest themselves in the same way: red blotchy skin, facial swelling and puffiness around the eyes, impaired breathing and a rapid pulse. Get the patient to hospital as rapidly as possible. If the patient remains conscious, help them to find the most comfortable position for breathing freely. If unconscious, put the patient in the recovery position (see page 127–8).

Bites from venomous snakes are treated by laying the casualty down with the bite at the lowest possible level. Wash the wound as well as you are able and keep the patient as calm and still as possible while help is summoned. Identification of the snake is a help but do not put yourself at risk in order to do so. Never apply a tourniquet, cut the wound or try to suck out the poison.

## Blisters

Blisters are there for a reason: the liquid they contain serves to protect and cool the wound. This is the body's way of coping with an injury such as a friction burn and no attempt should be made to drain a blister. Instead, cover the blister with gauze pads and tape or plasters. If the blister has burst by itself *do not* remove the broken skin, as this will only leave a delicate, unprotected area. Cover the area with plenty of padding. The key to both blister prevention and blister treatment is prompt action: there is no point in hoping that the pain will go away if you keep walking.

Do not forget that blisters can be caused by badly fitting, inadequate or damp socks, so carry spare socks. Another item that is well worth carrying (if you can justify the weight) is a pair of thongs or flip-flops so that you can get out of your boots in the evening and let your feet relax. Look after your feet and they will look after you.

# Appendix

## Main hostel organizations

### Australia
Backpackers Resorts
PO Box 1000
Bryon Bay
NSW 2481
Telephone 018 66 6888
Fax 066 85 8777

### Canada
Backpackers Hostels
Longhouse Village
RR13, Thunder Bay
Ontario
Telephone 807 983-2042
Fax 807 983-2914

### Great Britain
IHG, Sam Dalley
16 Uphill Road South
Uphill
Weston-Super-Mare
Avon BS23 4SG
(booklet containing details of hostels in
England, Scotland and Wales, £1.50)

### Ireland
IHH Office
UCD Village
Belfield
Dublin 4
Telephone 01 260 1634
Fax 01 269 7704

### New Zealand
VIP Backpackers Resorts of New Zealand
Ltd
Box 991
Taupo
Telephone/Fax 07-3771157

### Scotland
Scottish Budget Accommodation
Directory
STB
23 Ravelstone Terrace
Edinburgh EH4 3EU

The Secretary
IBH Scotland
13 Lower Breakish
Isle of Skye IV42 8QA

### USA
Kalispell/Whitefish Hostel
2155 Whitefish Stage Road
Kalispell
Montana 59901
Telephone 406 757-1908

American Association of International
Hostels (AAIH)
761 Mina Street
San Francisco
California 94103
Telephone 415 861-6634
Fax 415 241-0515

Jim's Backpackers Bible
PO Box 5650
Santa Monica
California 904909

# Other organizations

**France**
Fédération Française de la Randonnée
Pédestre
64 rue de Gergovie
F–75014
Paris

**Great Britain**
Backpackers Club
PO Box 38
71 Friar Street
Reading
Berkshire RG3 4RL

Long Distance Walkers Association
Membership Secretary
117 Higher Lane
Rainford
St Helens
Merseyside WA11 8BQ

Ramblers Assiciation
1–5 Wandsworth Road
London SW8 2XX

Ramblers Association – Scotland
Crusader House
Haig Business Park
Markinch
Fife KY7 6AQ

Ramblers Association – Wales
Pantwood
Pant Lane
Marford
Wrexham
Clywd LL12 8SG

Ulster Federation of Rambling Clubs
274 Belfast Road
Dundonald
Belfast BT16 0UE

**Italy**
Federazione Italiana Escursionismo
Via la Spezia 58 R
I–16149 Genova–Sampierdarena

**New Zealand**
New Zealand Walkway Commision
Dept of Conservation
PO Box 10420
Wellington

**USA**
American Hiking Society
PO Box 20160
Washington DC 20041

Sierra Club
730 Polk Street
San Francisco
California 94109

In addition most long distance trails and paths will have their own associations, the addresses of which will easily be found in tourist information departments or local guidebooks. These associations will often have more up-to-date information than that held in the guides.

# Index

Page numbers in *italics* indicate illustrations